D1701645

overnight sensations
ASIA PACIFIC

TAKE A DEEP BREATH AND INDULGE YOURSELF IN A FAVOURITE MEMORY. Did you feel your mood lighten? Did you smile? Did the tension in your shoulders release for a moment? It's not surprising. After all, that memory probably represents a wonderful experience in your life. And those feelings are what have been captured in this book. But we've done more than create a beautiful coffee table book, we've crafted an anthology of unforgettable experiences that only the world's finest destinations can provide.

Divided into five chapters: island, jungle, countryside, city, and beach, *Overnight Sensations – Asia Pacific* is a showcase of exquisite places to stay ranging from the quaintest inns to the most exclusive holiday resorts imaginable. Every one of these magnificent destinations has been thoroughly researched, scrutinised, and evaluated by our team before it is invited to become a part of the Kiwi Collection. Far less than one percent of all places to stay in the world are ever considered. Even fewer are invited.

At Kiwi Collection we describe our passion for travel as one might for fine cuisine, fine wine, fine art and architecture. In fact, through years of travel we have come to understand that, done well, the business of overnight hospitality is in fact a delicate fusion of all four disciplines. And, to us the creation of an exquisite travel destination and the experience such a property can provide is a masterwork in its own right.

Like any connoisseur with an obsession for the exceptional, we love to share what we have learned with our friends, our families, and other travellers with a palette for travelling that is as mature as our own. When you take the time to enjoy this publication in concert with our website, you will discover what many of the most discriminating travellers in the world already know – Kiwi Collection is the premier source of intimate and unbiased information and insight into the most exquisite places to stay on the planet regardless of size or affiliation.

Whether these pages are portraits of places you have stayed in the past or portals into the holidays of your wildest dreams, one thing is certain: every travel destination brought to life on these pages is without question a masterpiece.

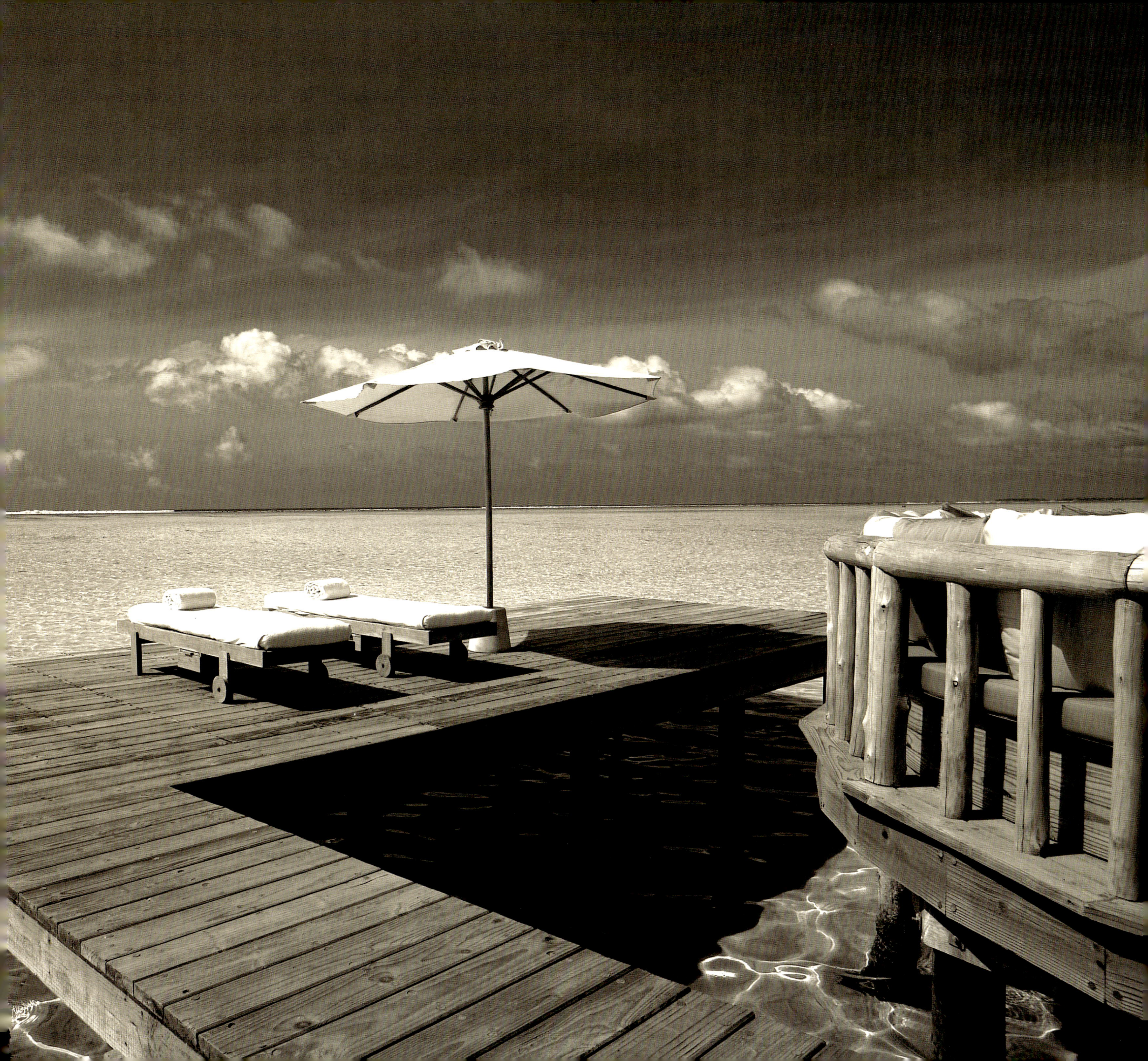

contents

ISLAND

COUNTRYSIDE

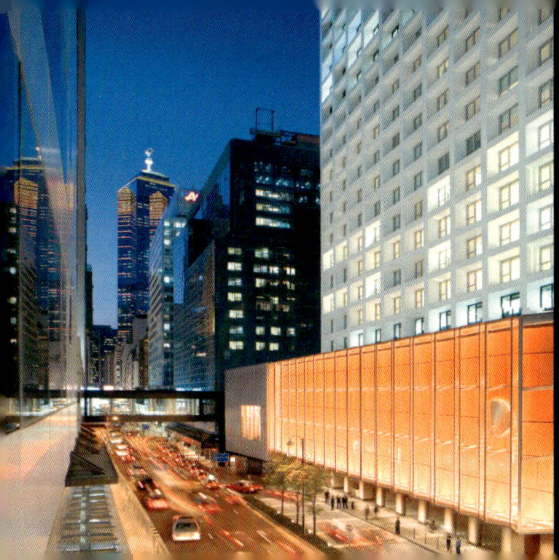
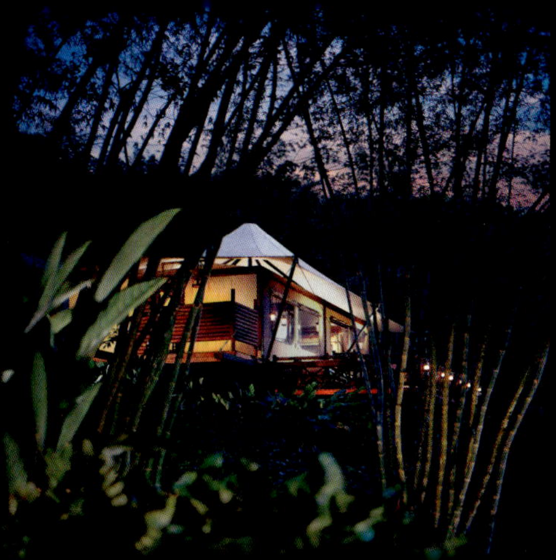
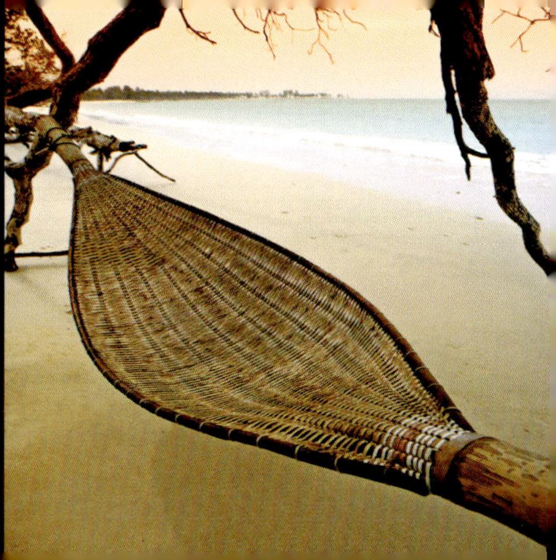

ISLAND

Voyages Bedarra Island Resort | GREAT BARRIER REEF, QUEENSLAND | AUSTRALIA

Yesterday's deadlines are forgotten, your mobile phone is switched off. You have disappeared into your exclusive Barrier Reef island hideaway in the treetops of Bedarra Island. Today it's just you, a chequered rug, a picnic hamper, and a secluded bay. The snow white sand is like powder beneath your bare feet, the sun warm on your face leaves a trail of freckles. As the sun begins to dip in the west you make your way back to your sheltered villa. Hidden from the world, you stand on your wooden balcony looking out through the treetops, to the bay and the ocean beyond, alive with a rainbow of native birds. The ice already has been delivered with a sunset canapé tray. Now all that remains is for you to slip into your swimsuit, mix your favourite cocktail, and slide into your infinity edge plunge pool. And relax as you watch the sun sink at the end of another perfect day.

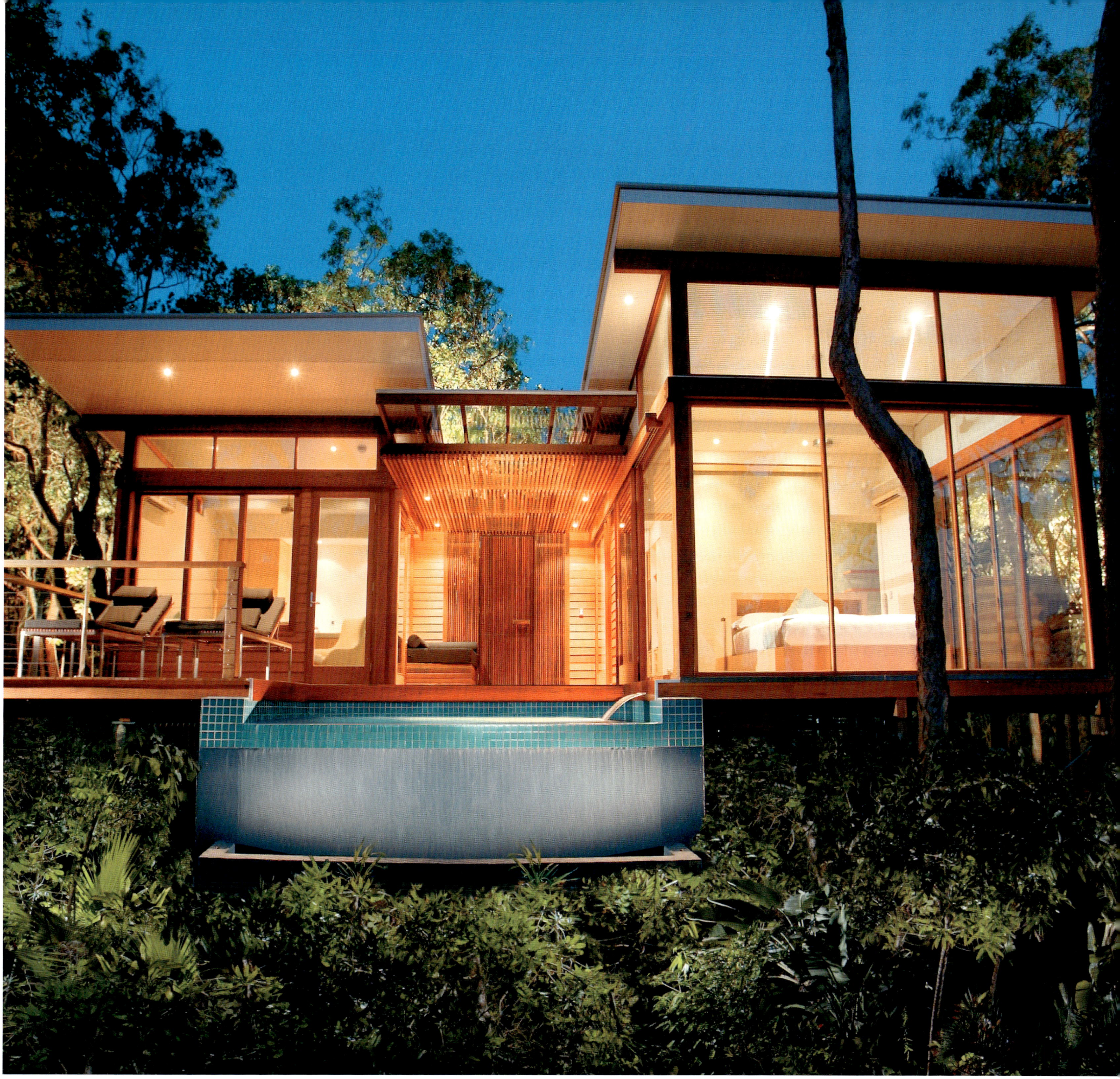

One&Only Kanuhura | LHAVIYANI ATOLL | MALDIVES

Salute! You raise a long frosted glass to the sparkling sky. Your laptop pings, "You've got mail." You switch off the offensive mod-con and close the lid. Sipping at a cool tropical concoction, you savour the tangy blend of fruit and alcohol. Your spouse holds the neatly typed vacation itinerary your PA diligently researched and planned for your trip to Kanuhura. Ignoring the timetable of activities, you tear the paper in two and toss it aside. You're lost somewhere in the Indian Ocean, just your spouse and yourself, on a beautiful remote coral atoll. Kicking off your flip-flops you dive, fully clothed, from your over-water bungalow into the crystal clear waters of the lagoon below. Mask and snorkel splash into the water beside you, lovingly thrown by your partner, who also dive bombs off the sundeck. Here, in this tropical paradise, time moves to a slower, more personal beat.

Bora Bora Lagoon Resort & Spa | BORA BORA | FRENCH POLYNESIA

Yesterday, in traditional Tahitian style you were married. You will always remember the moment you looked deep into your partner's eyes as you stood on the secluded beach dressed in customary Tahitian wedding garments of white silk sarongs. The magnetic blue waters of the lagoon lapped at the shore and the remnants of the old volcano stood, majestic, against the clear blue sky. The unforgettable vibrant colours of the Polynesian dancers, the hypnotic beat of the drum, and the cries of the ceremonial warrior still echo with the melodic incantations of the tahuia. Today, you are sitting on the bottom of the resort's free-form freshwater pool, mask on, breathing deeply through the mouthpiece attached to the air tank on your back, as you practice your scuba diving. Your partner gives you the thumbs up and smiles. Tomorrow, you will both sink beneath the crystal blue waters of the lagoon in a magical dive to explore the unknown.

The Racha | KOH RACHA YAI | THAILAND

To the Manager: I came to The Racha to complete the manuscript my editor was hounding me to finish. It was also important for me to spend time with my darling child. I want to thank you for all the considerate touches your staff provided. While I typed away on my laptop on the sundeck, S floated lazily in the infinity edge swimming pool; we were both blown away by the view over the turquoise waters of the Andaman Sea. The outdoor rain shower was a special treat for S, who hadn't experienced anything as invigorating before. We both deliberated over which bath products to use and I especially enjoyed sitting in the bath overlooking the water. The goodnight wishes, placed on our pillows at the end of each beautiful sunny day, made us feel very special indeed. Neither of us can decide which was our most favourite moment…

Hotel Bora Bora | BORA BORA | FRENCH POLYNESIA

Today, your Hotel Bora Bora activities director has arranged for a "shark and ray feeding". First, you will be picked up by boat and escorted to shallow waters to watch the feeding of stingrays. Apparently, you can jump right into the water with the stingrays and even touch them. One hotel guest informed you that when he went only a few days previously he was, at one time, surrounded by eight stingrays. "They were a lot of fun," he said, "and not as dangerous as you may think." You'll just have to take his word for that. Besides it's not the stingrays you are thinking about as much as the sharks. After feeding the rays, the boat then will take you out to deeper waters to watch the black tip sharks come out to feed. Word is that they too are harmless, but a shark is still a shark.

ISLAND 13

W Retreat & Spa Maldives | NORTH ARI ATOLL | MALDIVES

You've been cast away. Forgotten, on this deserted stretch of golden sand. Your easel stands in the shade beside the red and yellow striped hammock that sways between the bent trunks of two coconut trees. At the waters edge, a baby sea turtle playfully nudges a bright orange starfish that contracts and shimmers in affront. Both pose naturally as you capture their likeness in oil on canvas. Squeezing several tubes of paint onto your palette, you blend until you achieve that exact shade of glowing orange. Small waves gently rock against the shore, sparkling jade waters dramatically become a deep sapphire where the ocean floor drops away; all captured for eternity on canvas. The sound of ice tinkling softly intrudes on your beach idle. Turning, you observe your spouse, on the sun deck of your beachfront hideaway at the W Retreat & Spa, mixing mango, lychee, and rum. It's cocktail time.

Jean-Michel Cousteau Fiji Islands Resort | VANUA LEVU ISLAND | FIJI

You packed up your family and stepped off the edge of the world; free falling, you landed in a former coconut plantation somewhere in the South Pacific. At least, that's how your children felt when they first arrived at the thatched roof bungalow overlooking Savusavu Bay. Here, there are no phones or TVs in any of the rooms and their mobile phones and laptop have been locked away in the bottom of your suitcase. You had to double dare the youngest into activity at the beginning of the week. Now, you barely recognise the freckle faced sun kissed sea urchins as they run to your side, euphoric after their afternoon underwater adventure. Tonight, you'll be entertained with tales of neon sea monsters, and the need to preserve the delicate ecosystem of the coral reef, all gleaned from their adventure guide, the resort's resident marine biologist. As your children have discovered an affinity for the environment, you have re-discovered them.

Anantara Resort Maldives | SOUTH MALÉ ATOLL | MALDIVES

When you first checked in to the Anantara Resort Maldives, you were surprised to hear about its stylish showcase library. Why would an island spa resort, surrounded by azure waters and tropical terrain, have need for such an exquisite library? But that was five days ago; before the daytrip to Malé, the snorkelling excursion that wasn't nearly as frightening as anticipated, a rather interesting picnic on the golden sands of a private island, two early morning yoga classes, and one rather tasty cooking class (who knew traditional Maldivian cuisine was so inspired?). Now here you are, sunk into a plush leather armchair with the biggest book you could find on the shelves, and the idea of a library at an island resort is starting to make sense. Cool, tranquil, and no need for sunscreen. Ingenious.

The Boatshed | WAIHEKE ISLAND, NORTH ISLAND | NEW ZEALAND

The red and green sails of the boat pull tight in the wind as the sleek vessel glides over the glassy surface of Oneroa Bay. The scene is set for your romantic getaway; today you are the lighthouse keepers. From the private sun deck of your lighthouse retreat you enjoy a lazy breakfast: your spouse sips freshly squeezed orange juice, while you spread a thick dollop of jam over another warm sweet-roll. The whitewashed timber walls of the lighthouse glow in the sunlight, the colours of the seascape reflected in the natural tones of the furnishings inside. Later, you stroll hand-in-hand through the seaside village discovering the art galleries and hidden speciality shops. Your driftwood and seashell collection grows as you explore the shore together. You return to your secret hideaway at The Boatshed in the late afternoon, where you cuddle together on the balcony and watch as the sailboat races the setting sun back to its berth.

Soneva Gili & Six Senses Spa | NORTH MALÉ ATOLL | MALDIVES

Moonlight reflects off the lagoon as you blow water from your snorkel and paddle back to your thatched Robinson Crusoe Villa, on stilts, in the middle of the lagoon. Brightly coloured fish flash like quicksilver through the coral reef below. You haul yourself from the water and then assist your partner up the stairs to the candlelight swimming deck. Ignoring the light supper, you reach for two glasses of champagne. Your partner begins to giggle; following a pointing finger you sigh. "Hmmm. We're stranded in paradise. Just you and me darling until someone comes looking for us." Laughing you both watch as your only link to the island and civilisation, a rowboat, slowly drifts across the lagoon towards the sandy shore. "I guess we'll try spear fishing after all."

Double Island | PALM COVE, QUEENSLAND | AUSTRALIA

It's been quite a year. Taking the company public was no small feat. After all, no man is an island, which is why you've invited 40 of your top executives to join you on this once-in-a-lifetime celebration at private Double Island. If anyone deserves to rule over this tropical empire, it's this hardworking group. And you couldn't have picked a better place – a deluxe game room, luxury safari-like suites, an outdoor spa, a heated swimming pool, and walking trails with dramatic views of the Coral Sea. When your crew takes over the beach for a rowdy barbeque party, you join in with full abandon. A movie screening in the large cinema underneath the stars winds down the night. You fall asleep even before the credits roll, happy in the knowledge that all is right with your world. Now you can rest.

Naladhu Maldives | SOUTH MALÉ ATOLL | MALDIVES

Awakened by the sound of an ice cube hitting the side of your glass, it takes you a moment to remember where you are. Reassured by the gentle calm of the ocean, you are reminded that this is one place where the paparazzi won't find you. Rolling over, you notice that your very own House Master has placed a cocktail on the table beside you, its deep pink perfection contrasted by the magnificent azure sky behind it. This liquid pre-dinner delight is a reminder that your specially prepared meal will be served on your private deck in one hour, just as the sun is setting, as you requested. Rising from your day bed, you plunge into your private pool, its edge a meeting point for the horizon, Indian Ocean, and sky. All at once, you realise that to get away from it all, didn't mean you couldn't have it all.

KIWICOLLECTION.COM

ISLAND 21

Royal Davui Island Resort, Fiji | BEQA LAGOON | FIJI

From the moment you entered the door of your villa at Royal Davui Fiji, you were in awe. The entry way had a glass wall with a view of the ocean that was simply stunning. Right away it was apparent one could be quite content never leaving the room; that is, if one were so inclined. The room had everything anyone could want - a fully stocked wet bar complete with cookies and fresh fruit, a phone for room service, and a CD player. From the sitting room a deck led to your own private plunge pool. On the other side of the villa was the bedroom. And your favourite feature? Definitely the two person jetted bathtub under a louvred ceiling. Simply push a button and the louvres open. From the bathtub, you can look up and see the stars.

KIWICOLLECTION.COM

Cocoa Island | MAKUNUFUSHI | MALDIVES

This week's extreme adventure? Wreck diving off the Maldives. With an underwater visibility of 20-metres, you were able to see the 110-metre sunken cargo ship, Victory, as soon as you began descending toward her. In fact, you had already reached the main mast after diving only 12-metres deep. You were enthralled by your surroundings – and who wouldn't be? Swimming in and out of the large holds, through wide corridors, and down several staircases that were once part of a majestic ship but were now home to a bevy of beautiful fish, coral, sea turtles, and other marine animals was an experience you will not soon forget. And one you can replay over and over while sunning by the pool at your resort, Cocoa Island.

Hayman | GREAT BARRIER REEF, QUEENSLAND | AUSTRALIA

Tomorrow is the day you have most been looking forward to since you arrived at Hayman just less than a week ago. Sure, snorkelling, hiking, and sun bathing have all been great, but it's tomorrow's adventure for which, really, you've been waiting. The day will consist of a half day of game fishing, on a privately chartered boat, in the waters surrounding Hayman. The waters are reputed to provide some of the best fishing in the world – fish caught continuously setting Australian and international world records, or so you have been told. With a hired hand, state-of-the-art fishing equipment, and the bait and tackle all prearranged, it seems that catching a fish is almost a sure thing. Okay, maybe that is being a little optimistic, but still, things really are looking good.

Taj Exotica Resort & Spa Maldives | SOUTH MALÉ ATOLL | MALDIVES

Your eyes blink open. Without thinking you swing your legs silently off the bed careful not to disturb the warm and wonderful body beside you. Stepping onto the veranda of your deluxe lagoon villa you are surrounded by the sea on all sides. You take a deep breath of the fragrant ocean air and exhale into the pale blue light of dawn. With a sense of security that only the absolutely privacy can offer, you drop your house coat and dip your toe into the lagoon. The 80°F water laps gently at your toes. Satisfied, you step onto the top wrung of the ladder and feel the warm water encapsulate your feet. As you are about to dive the two empty champagne flutes on the table beside you catch your eye. Pausing, you smile. Ahhh Champagne, you think to yourself, works every time.

Amanpulo | PAMALICAN ISLAND | PHILIPPINES

From the moment you checked into the Aman lounge at Manilla airport you knew you were in for something very special. On arriving on Pamalican Island, you were greeted by the Amanpulo staff and whisked away on a golf cart for a quick tour of the island before reaching your beach casita with its own short private path to the beach. And what a beach it was! The whitest sand you had ever seen set against a clear ocean that glistened from the palest green to the deepest turquoise. You could wake up in the morning and walk from your room right to the reef to snorkel! Back at the casita, wall-to-wall windows provided a spectacular view of the water and neighbouring islands. And outside, a large deck with two day beds and a hammock, all in private surrounds, made for a fantastic daily "happy hour".

Taprobane Island | TAPROBANE ISLAND | SRI LANKA

Taprobane Island is the most extraordinary hotel in which you have ever stayed. Although to be fair, it seems nothing like a hotel in the traditional sense of the word, but rather more like a gracious and luxurious private residence to which you just happened to have been invited. Taprobane Island avoids the clichés and suburban aspirations of the tropical hotel experience, but has all of the drama and mystique just the same. Daylight is filtered through 9 metre high taffeta curtains in a weight of delft-blue silk rarely seen outside Versailles, creating a cool northern light of elegance and discretion. This same degree of attention to detail carries throughout the property, from the aromatic cinnamon shower gel to chic contemporary art. There is a hidden infinity pool in a jungle setting, with orchid strewn branches dipping into the water. The staff and service are charming - but practically invisible - creating a feeling of total serenity and privacy. Possibly the most perfect place to stay.

Amanwana | WEST SUMBAWA REGENCY, MOYO ISLAND | INDONESIA

The 55-minute flight from Bali to Sumbawa Besar on a six seat twin-engine Cessna provided a spectacular view of Indonesia's archipelago and, in particular, of your destination, Amanwana on Moyo Island. At the Sumbawa airport, a gentleman from the hotel was there to greet you and lead you to the boat that would take you to your much anticipated island retreat. Arriving at the resort, you again were warmly greeted and quickly led to your own private luxury tent, set deep within a tropical forest canopy. After a refreshing night's sleep (if this is camping, count me in), you are wide awake and ready to take on a day of sightseeing, Indonesian style - a speed boat and jeep await to take you to natural waterfalls and their pools deep in the heart of Moyo Island.

KIWICOLLECTION.COM

Banyan Tree Maldives Vabbinfaru | NORTH MALÉ ATOLL | MALDIVES

The shutter on the camera snaps closed capturing for eternity this moment in time. You wonder how a day that dawned so promisingly bright and sunny could end with you kissing the biggest, cunningly intelligent, slippery fish in the Indian Ocean? Yesterday, you were a swashbuckling privateer, on a double masted Turkish Gullet, coasting across the waters surrounding Vabbinfaru, toasting the high seas with your fellow buccaneers as the salty air filled your lungs. Now, you raise your prize catch from your deep-sea fishing adventure high, for another click of the camera, and smooch wet lips, grateful when the skipper relieves you of the fish. Tonight you'll barbecue on the beach, with the assistance of the chef, of course, and enjoy your prize catch beneath the stars. Tomorrow you promise yourself, there will be no kissing any white tipped sharks or other exotic marine creatures while you explore the coral reef.

Huvafen Fushi | NORTH MALÉ ATOLL | MALDIVES

From the moment you awoke on this island paradise with your partner you both have been living your fantasies: the sun drenched blue of the sky overhead that appears more radiant when in contrast to the brilliant white of the sandy beach, the crystal clarity of the turquoise blue water of the lagoon as it laps against the posts of your bungalow, a serene melody as you watch the gulls sweep across the Indian Ocean from your sun deck. Only in your dreams had you imagined indulging in holistic treatments with your partner, below the ocean; surrounded by aqua waters, colourful corals, and schools of fish mesmerising with their electric blue and yellow stripes. At the Aquum Spa your dreams became a reality as you are rejuvenated, in their underwater therapy room, by the Couples Touch Therapy Treatment. There is just one more fantasy. An intimate table for two on a deserted rock island; candles glowing, gossamer sails fluttering in the evening breeze.

Voyages Lizard Island | GREAT BARRIER REEF, QUEENSLAND | AUSTRALIA

A chronic note-taker and list-maker, you pull out a piece of paper and pen, pour yourself a glass of red wine and sit down at the kitchen table. At the top of the page you write "Things to do next week during my stay at Voyages Lizard Island". The rest is easy. 1. Catch up on sleep: late mornings, naps, and anything in between. 2. Tour local, islands by private boat. Find a deserted beach. Take a picnic and bottle of wine and stake your claim. 3. Get at least one treatment at the Azure Spa; preferably something that involves a foot massage. 4. Snorkel. It is after all, the Great Barrier Reef. 5. Eat and drink as much as you wish. Isn't that the point of vacations? 6. No more lists for an entire week.

Pacific Resort Aitutaki | AITUTAKI | COOK ISLANDS

About 200 yards to starboard, powerful blue waves rise high above the brightly coloured reef and slam back into the sea with a thunderous roar. But here, within the protective sanctuary of the Aitutaki Lagoon's inner reefs, the ocean is calm and quiet - but still putting on quite a performance. It seems to change colours right before your very eyes, as massive schools of brightly hued tropical fish dash back and forth beneath the boat. You pick up a tiny morsel of bait, pinch it between your fingers, and dunk your hand beneath the opal surface of the sea. As if on cue, a precocious parrotfish nips the offering gently from your finger tips as two more zip over to see if any bait has been left behind. No, not this time. But these clever fish have seen this boat before and they know that, any second now, you'll be reaching down to offer them some more.

Dhoni Mighili | NORTH ARI ATOLL | MALDIVES

Sure, your trip at Dhoni Mighili includes a beach bungalow on the coral sand beach, but you've decided it's better to spend most of the time on your private Dhoni, a 65ft. traditional handcrafted Maldivian sailboat. It's only two days into the trip, but already Abu, your Thakuru (i.e., private butler), knows what will please you: your penchant for morning dives, when manta rays feed in the early light; a preference for almond soap and goose down pillows. When you mention a love for cello music, a fresh selection is downloaded onto your Dhoni's iPod. Abu is there when you want him and not when you don't. Every evening a Pimm's is waiting on the deck, and, whether you like it or not, Veuve Clicquot is available 24/7. You like it. At the end of the trip, Abu says he hopes you bring lots of memories home. You will, but you'd rather bring Abu.

KIWICOLLECTION.COM

One&Only Maldives at Reethi Rah | NORTH MALÉ ATOLL | MALDIVES

Tonight, you'll dance beneath the stars poolside as the resident DJ plays the latest in entertainment. But first, you shake the sand from the bottom of your feet as you leave behind the sandy coastline at Reethi Rah, that stretches for over six kilometres, flanked by the turquoise waters of the Indian Ocean. Here the waters are so clear that each day you spend diving is another adventure in discovery, from the dramatic drop of the underwater cliffs to the bright colours of the coral reefs abounding with marine life. Inside your over-water villa, you connect your digital underwater camera to your laptop and the colourful images flash onto the screen. The photo of a giant Manta Ray is followed by that of a playful White Tip Reef shark as it lazily waves its fin at your camera. The cheeky turtle, that swam circles around you, is immortalised in your electronic postcard sent to your friends and wannabe Robinson Crusoes.

Le Taha'a Private Island & Spa | TAHA'A | FRENCH POLYNESIA

You sneak from your beach villa, carefully tiptoe past the children listening intently to the babysitter's story about a whale who followed a mermaid through the coral reef into the lagoon at Le Taha'a. Outside, the evening breeze is redolent with vanilla and mystery. You skirt the softly lapping waves at the water's edge and follow the shore to a secluded cove. A figure steps from the shadows of the coconut grove as you approach. Your heart beats rapidly. The moon slides from behind a cloud illuminating the smiling face of your spouse. "You managed to escape the Grandkids then?" After a morning of wave chasing and collecting seashells, an afternoon spent exploring the local watermelon and vanilla farms, and an evening game of tennis beneath the stars you are both exhausted. Smiling, you groan as you realise the little devils undoubtedly will rise early tomorrow eager to be off whale watching.

Soneva Fushi & Six Senses Spa | NORTH BAA ATOLL | MALDIVES

Above me, the sun shines brightly in the azure blue sky as white clouds lazily drift by. To either side, the endless white sandy beach glows golden in the sunlight: deserted, unmarred, with the exception of the solitary trail of footprints leading to my spot of beach meditation. Behind me, my three children splash and laugh, as they play in the private pool, before jumping out to chase each other around their 'tree-house', as they call our villa at Soneva Fushi. Watched over by the friendly competent sitter, provided by the hotel, it's their favourite place to holiday. Ahead of me, the crystal waters darken from turquoise to aqua, the gentle slap of the tide against the shore is a lullaby to my nerves. Far on the horizon, my partner balances awkwardly on a windsurfer trying to haul the sail out of the surf, again! Oh well, not this vacation; maybe next year when we return.

Pangkor Laut Resort | PANGKOR LAUT | MALAYSIA

You're Robinson Crusoe with an unfair advantage, a castaway with more perks than a prince. True to legend, there's an unspoilt island with white sands, turquoise seas, and endless sunshine. What's lacking is the challenge of survival. You try to imagine paradise with a jagged edge. But you can't, not here, not at Pangkor Laut Resort. This is paradise, pure and simple. Today, you're going to snooze the morning away in a hammock beneath coconut palms on Emerald Beach. When the afternoon heat fades, you'll catch your own fish for dinner. Then as dusk gathers, you'll sit on the verandah of your villa, hovering on stilts over limpid waters, and watch another tangerine sunset. What about tomorrow? Forage in the rainforest or relax in the spa? Build a raft or have a massage? Being marooned is full of difficult choices. Except, of course, when the rescue boat arrives to take you home. Then you know exactly what to do. Hide.

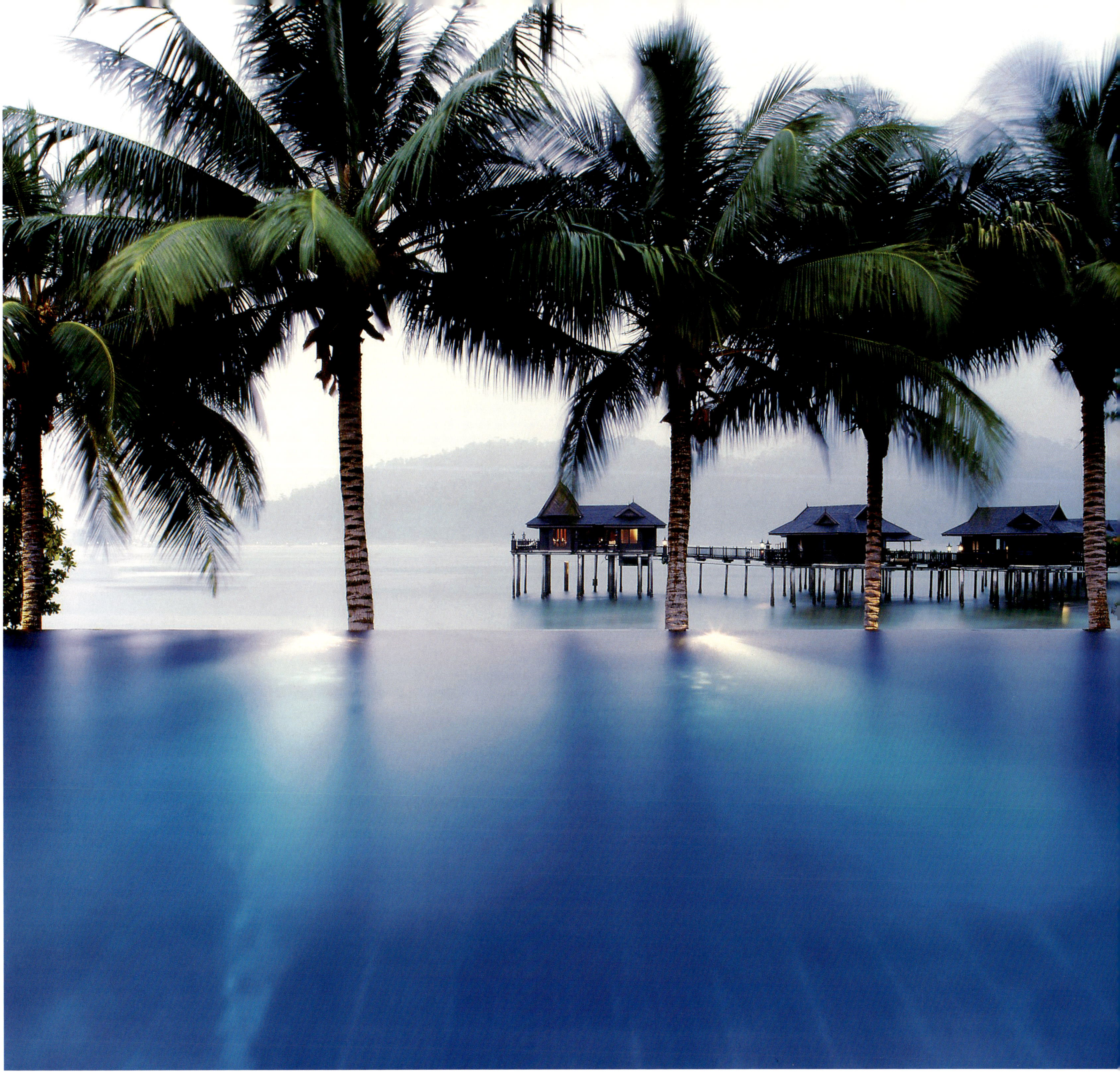

KIWICOLLECTION.COM

Four Seasons Resort Maldives at Kuda Huraa | NORTH MALÉ ATOLL | MALDIVES

"Welcome to Malé Island, ladies and gentlemen. It is a perfect 88°F with clear skies and calm winds," observes the pilot as his plane eases to a halt. Moments later a gentleman in a crisp white uniform skips skillfully through the crowd towards you. "Welcome, welcome," he says with a smile. How does he know your name you wonder? But before you have a chance to ask, you and your partner are whisked away by private car and then ushered aboard a beautiful speedboat waiting in the harbour. As you glide effortlessly across the turquoise water, you can see the iridescent white sand beach arcing on the horizon and a series of grey thatched roofs branching into the sea. As the boat slows you feel a delicate hand grip your shoulder and hear a familiar voice whisper into your ear, "Oh my goodness, is this where we're staying?" You don't need to answer; the smile on your face says it all.

Rayavadee | AMPHUR MUANG | THAILAND

These are the instructions: Get to Bangkok. Take another plane to Krabi. From there, a speedboat will pick you up. Bring as much or little luggage as you like; the crew on the boat will handle it all for you. You'll be taken to Rayavadee. Before you go in; however, check out the beaches. There are three of them, and they're all pristine and white, surrounded by limestone cliffs and turquoise water. Wild monkeys, birdlife, spectacular coral reefs revealing themselves under the transparent sea; we'll have plenty of time to visit all of this. Back at the hotel, ask to be shown to the Rayavadee Villa. It's the one with the fabulous view of Phra Nang beach. Very secluded. Knock three times and enter. I'll be waiting for you in the free-form swimming pool. Or maybe the jacuzzi, I'm not sure. The champagne will be cooling.

Capella Lodge | LORD HOWE ISLAND, NEW SOUTH WALES | AUSTRALIA

On the edge of the Pacific Ocean the cool sea breeze ruffles your hair. Fluffy white clouds chase each other across the dazzling blue sky and turquoise waters ripple in the shallows along the shore, the deserted golden beach stretching towards the horizon. As you luxuriate in the hot tub on your exclusive sun deck, you watch clouds drape the top of the distant volcanic mountain peaks. When your partner invited you to escape to paradise at Capella Lodge you never imagined anywhere could be this perfect. As your partner steps from the private boardwalk onto the wraparound verandah, you pour effervescent champagne into twin flutes. The complimentary beach bag and snorkel gear is forgotten as your partner enthusiastically describes the bright jewels that lie beneath the crystal surface of the ocean, a reef vibrating with colour and life. You smile and sip champagne, with your partner, looking out over Lover's Bay.

The Rania Experience | FAAFU ATOLL | MALDIVES

Your work demands that you make important decisions. You've reluctantly accepted compliments from your peers, who celebrate you as one of the best decision makers in the business. You find that even on holiday, you can't escape making decisions. The decision to enjoy The Rania Experience wasn't difficult. The exclusive use of the Private Island and sea cruiser would ensure that the stresses of work quickly would dissolve. Though, more decisions remain. Will you stay on the island tonight, in your lavish Villa Suite, or at sea, and sleep above the azure waters of Faafu Atoll? This evening, would you prefer to dine under the moonlit pavilion, by the pool, or on the pristine sands of the island's private beach? Tomorrow, should you have the Thai or Ayurvedic massage from the island's exclusive Ayur Spa? Making a decision has never been so difficult. You decide to stay another week so you can experience it all.

KIWICOLLECTION.COM

ISLAND 43

COUNTRYSIDE

Voyages Longitude 131° | AYERS ROCK, NORTHERN TERRITORY | AUSTRALIA

If someone had told you a year ago that you would be "camping" in Australia on your honeymoon, you would have laughed in their face. Now, you can't stop telling anyone who will listen about your fantastic honeymoon experience sleeping in tents in the Australian outback. Of course, the truth of the matter is, you stayed at Voyages Longitude 131° and, yes, you may have stayed in a "tent" of sorts, but certainly not in the traditional sense. The tents at Longitude 131° were the height of luxury: a domed roof draped in white flowing fabric created the illusion of a camping tent; but one with lighting, air conditioning, powered window blinds, a king size bed, and a sunrise view. So now your new spouse cannot say that you have never camped, although, having set the bar so high, it is unlikely you ever will again.

The Sentosa Resort & Spa | SINGAPORE | SINGAPORE

The natural momentum of your swing drives the ball onto the green of the 18th hole of the championship golf course at Sentosa Golf Club. You've almost made it; once you reach the 19th hole, you'll be back at The Sentosa Resort and only minutes from your garden villa where you can celebrate your successful round with chilled champagne. You can feel the tension in your shoulders and the tightness in your hips as you square up for the final shot. A result of the closely slogged out tennis match earlier that day, perhaps. Or maybe, it was the mountain biking, yesterday, through the tropical woodlands and waterfalls surrounding the resort. You know just the cure, a Four Hands Massage at Spa Botanica, followed by a relaxing volcanic mud bath treatment to sooth your skin after a day spent outdoors in the fresh air.

Kishoan | MATSUMOTO | JAPAN

The day was spent touring the famous Matsumoto Castle, Matsumotojo. Built on a plain rather than on a mountain or hill, it is reputed to be one of the most complete and aesthetically well maintained of Japan's original castles and, although you have not yet had the chance to visit enough of the country's ancient castles to be able to verify this reputation, you can certainly attest to its aesthetic beauty and old world charm. Excited by your foray into exploring Japanese culture as a full-fledged (but well educated) tourist, you sit at the lounge of Kishoan and thumb through various activities flyers and magazines for other things to do. Nagano. Well this looks interesting - a scenic, mountainous voyage into the Japanese Alps. Later this week, perhaps?

KIWICOLLECTION.COM

Amanjiwo | BOROBUDUR, JAVA | INDONESIA

Amanjiwo has quickly moved to the top of the list of favourite hotels, ever since you and your family were fortunate enough to spend five nights in this paradise. This complement is not given lightly - you have stayed at some of the finest hotels and resorts all over the world - and Amanjiwo remains your favourite. So what did you do this time around? Well, let's see: there was the sunrise at Borbudur, for which hotel staff arranged your early arrival (at least an hour before everyone else); there was the day trip to town, after which the four of you returned by elephant (the highlight of the trip for your son); and then there were the cooking classes, the trance dance in a local village, and a private meditation in a local Buddhist temple. Not to mention some good old fashioned rest and relaxation while the kids were whisked away for their own activities.

KIWICOLLECTION.COM

Commune by the Great Wall Kempinski | THE GREAT WALL, BEIJING | CHINA
All your business trips have blurred into one long, tedious journey. With every country, every city you visit, all you can recall is a dreary kaleidoscope of boardrooms and airport terminals. You promise that this trip will be different. Arriving at Commune, business is the last thing on your mind. The rooms are a study in architectural precision. The sweeping views over the Shuiguan Valley and of the Great Wall require later exploration. It would be easy to spend hours just exploring the hotel, but you're scheduled for a meeting in the next half hour. With a view overlooking some of China's most captivating scenery and with the finest state-of-the-art business amenities, your partners will no doubt come to you. The presentation goes perfectly. Never has a meeting space inspired so much synergy and cooperation. You walk the hotel's private path leading to the Great Wall as if in a trance. Mission more than accomplished.

COUNTRYSIDE 51

Tosen Goshobo | KOBE | JAPAN

You are a well-heeled traveller, and more to the point, a well-heeled diner. That is to say, you have the distinct reputation (self-appointed, perhaps) of having eaten in some of the best restaurants in the world. But until now, believe it or not, there is one dining experience you have not had the pleasure of adding to your repertoire – you have not actually dined on Kobe beef directly in Kobe, Japan. Obviously, you have had this legendary delicacy of Japan elsewhere across the globe, but that is not the same as having it right here in its home region. If possible, the beef is even better than you had expected. So well marbled is the meat that one could say it rivals foie gras for its richness (not to mention caloric intake, but alas, when in Rome...). With one new experience behind you, now you'll add another; a traditional Japanese outdoor bath – a speciality of this particular ryokan.

KIWICOLLECTION.COM

The Lodge at Tikana | SOUTHLAND, SOUTH ISLAND | NEW ZEALAND

With your eyes still closed you reach for your watch. You wait a moment until your vision is focused enough to distinguish the time. Ten o'clock. Ten o'clock! On the rare occasions that you allow yourself the luxury of sleeping late back home you're usually awakened early by the sound of traffic. Today, it is the aroma of fresh espresso coffee that wakes you. Slowly stretching, you delight in the thought that you have another week here at The Lodge at Tikana. As you walk to the window your feet are warmed by the heated floors. The view of the lush, green, rolling hills beyond is truly breathtaking. The neighing of a horse in the paddock before you is a reminder that soon you will be part of this panorama, horse riding through the fertile countryside. You fling open the bi-fold windows and inhale the cool, fresh country air. Its effect is immediately invigorating. You may not need that coffee after all.

Banyan Tree Lijiang | LIJIANG, YUNNAN PROVINCE | CHINA
As always, your wife was in charge of all travel research and bookings. And, as always, her decisions have been right on the mark. Research had indicated that early to mid December would be the ideal time to visit Lijiang, promising clear blue skies, crisply clean and cold air, and less of a crowd at the favourite tourist spots. A beacon of good taste, your wife chose Banyan Tree Lijiang, and as you are always a fan of the Banyan Tree chain, you were happy to accommodate. The villa you rented was immaculate and the resort restaurants offered excellent food, a welcome treat since there were many a night when the two of you simply did not feel adventurous enough to dine at the local restaurants in DaYan or ShuHe old towns.

Voyages Wrotham Park | WROTHAM PARK, QUEENSLAND | AUSTRALIA

Voyages Wrotham Park. Day Four. Arose to a sky so big and blue it made my eyes hurt. Morning spent mustering cattle, the herd of Brahma moving in a cloud across the landscape of red earth. Paused to watch a Great Egret, its giant wings casting a shadow, as it flew further into the outback. Day Five. Quad bike tour of the immense property, the hotel becoming a tiny but exquisite speck in the distance. Since Voyages accommodates only twenty guests at a time, you know you have the place pretty much to yourself (well, except for a few kangaroos, wallabies and goannas, and maybe several dozen species of birds). By Day 7 I had been canoeing, barramundi fishing, and horseback riding. On Day 8 I made a great discovery, perhaps the crowning achievement of my stay. An afternoon spent in the suite's leather armchair, overlooking the banks of the Mitchell River.

The Oberoi Udaivilas, Udaipur | UDAIPUR, RAJASTHAN | INDIA

After a week in the madness of Agra and Jaipur, when your car drops you off at a small quay for the boat trip over to Udaivilas, the sense of relaxation is palpable. Peace and tranquility reign at The Oberoi Udaivilis, one of the best located hotels you ever have visited. Everything about this hotel works well. The quality of the architecture and the craftsmanship is superb. Both of the restaurants serve high quality Indian and international food, with excellent live music in the evenings. As well as the private pools, there are two public pools, one with views extending over the lake. The spa also is high quality and the hotel shop is one of the best at which you have lightened your wallet. And upon staff suggestion, tomorrow you will hire a boat for a trip around the lake to take in all aspects of that spectacular view.

The Lodge at Kauri Cliffs | KERIKERI, NORTH ISLAND | NEW ZEALAND

Together you watch from the porch of your cottage at The Lodge at Kauri Cliffs, as the crimson sun sinks into the midnight blue depths of the Pacific Ocean, and the sounds of the wild birds settling in for the night fade to a murmur. Earlier today you stood arm-in-arm with your partner on the rolling deck of a sleek sailing yacht, the salty sea air fresh in your face as you explored the renowned Bay of Islands. Photos captured forever the happiness of your time spent in the sheltered bay; swimming in the chill of the Pacific, giggling like teenagers as you raced along the shore holding hands. You help your partner zip their jacket before shrugging into your own fleece. The experience has only just begun. At the Lodge, you meet the local specialist who will be your guide for this evening's adventure. Hand in hand, you are off to explore the natural habitat and experience the 'call' of the Kiwi in the wild.

COUNTRYSIDE 57

Cameron Highlands Resort | CAMERON HIGHLANDS | MALAYSIA

Cameron Highlands Resort is known as a trekkers haven. Throwing your bags down and flinging open the windows to your balcony, you can't wait to start on the famous Jim Thomson Trail. You strap on your shoes and meet the resident naturalist who will serve as your guide. It is a clear, crisp day, perfect for a vigorous climb. A two-hour hike should be easy for you, so when it turns out to be tricky terrain you're pleasantly surprised. Along the way, you cross crystal clear water streams, over logs, and endure some very steep climbs. Wild orchids, bright yellow flowers, and purple herbs used by the indigenous Orang Asli, dot your path. Stumbling into the plantation lodge, you walk straight to Spa Village for the post-hike Lapis-Lapis Malay Herbal Wrap, made from ginger, lemongrass, galangal, and camphor. The next day, you are completely renewed. Luckily, there are many more mountains to climb.

Moondance Lodge | MARGARET RIVER, WESTERN AUSTRALIA | AUSTRALIA

It's already past noon, and you still haven't gotten out of bed. The mysterious fragrance in your Blue Dolphin suite, the song of the Kookaburras outside your window, the paper at your feet, the view of the wild bush outside – why even bother getting up? If it wasn't for the wellness program, you wouldn't even try. But you're one of the high-strung, burned-out people who came here to rejuvenate and heal through the retreat's inspiring Master Teachers and therapeutic treatments. And what a journey it's been. The Didgeridoo Meditation, the Moondance Morning Zinger on the beach, the hot stone massage in the tree-top loft. Your creative juices are flowing again; your body humming along to the powerful vibrations of this magical sanctuary. A soft drum beats in the distant bush outside, or is that your heart? You rise to answer its call.

Phuket Pavilions | PHUKET | THAILAND

You've been covering every news story around the globe, so when your partner suggests a getaway for two, you think secluded and exotic. You think personalised service and spacious quarters. You think Phuket Pavilions. You step into your villa – all cool neutral concrete with glass and dashes of colour – and the buzzing of data, facts, names, and testimonials quiets down. You take advantage of the "no-tan-line" policy while lazing by your own infinity pool, enjoy the signature "42 movement sculpting facial" on your private pavillion, and dine on a menu of Thai cuisine in the total seclusion of your candle-lit terrace. Every harmonious detail is poised to help you recharge, soothe, and indulge the senses in complete and perfect solitude. After one trip into bustling Phuket, you decide to hide out in your villa for the duration of your stay. Why would anyone ever want to leave this sensual sanctuary?

KIWICOLLECTION.COM

Hyatt Coolum Ambassador Villas | SUNSHINE COAST, QUEENSLAND | AUSTRALIA
Let's face it - you enjoy the great outdoors as much as the next person (you are intrigued by interesting fauna, insects, and birds and you are adventurous enough to go out and discover these items on your own), but you do not intend to compromise on the comforts of home in order to experience the beauty the great outdoors has to offer. Luckily, it is for people just like you that a place such as the Hyatt Coolum Ambassador Villas exists. The grounds of the Hyatt Coolum are sprawled out – perfect for biking, or for walking past pretty lagoons and through the lightly forested areas, on your way to the beach pool. Of course, the resort itself offers all the amenities you would expect from an upscale Hyatt property.

Umaid Bhawan Palace | JODHPUR, RAJASTHAN | INDIA
After the long and exhausting car journey from Jaipur to Jodphur, entering the front gates and catching your first glimpse of the colossal grandeur of the Umaid Bhawan Palace was a most welcome sight. The hotel itself is the epitome of an Indian heritage resort, with enthralling architecture and opulently decorated interior space. And it only got better as you were personally greeted upon arrival with hot towels (very refreshing after hours in a car), flower leis, and fresh juice. You were then quietly escorted to a newly renovated wing that consists of the most gorgeous art deco suites. After settling in you dined at the Pillars on the terrace, quickly forgot all about the long journey that brought you here, and started enthusiastically planning the days ahead.

COUNTRYSIDE 63

The Byron at Byron Resort & Spa | BYRON BAY, NEW SOUTH WALES | AUSTRALIA

Finding a mutually acceptable location for the family summer holiday, with guaranteed nice weather, activities for all ages, and the luxurious amenities you have come to expect, can be tricky to say the least. Then a friend recommended The Byron at Byron Resort & Spa. Set within a 45-acre lush rainforest and offering golf, swimming, beach walks, and spa treatment, The Byron seems to be the solution for which you have been looking. The spacious one bedroom suite is well fitted, the food fantastic, and the plasma screen TV and easy Internet access are getting more use than you would have thought. And with the famous Tallow Beach just steps away, even your usually moody and unpredictable teenaged daughter seems to be having a good time – although, maybe too much of a good time.

Corstorphine House | DUNEDIN, SOUTH ISLAND | NEW ZEALAND

"Welcome to this magical mystery weekend at Corstorphine House," the note reads. "Last time we embarked on a Scottish flight of fancy. This time I invite you on an exotic Indian odyssey. Remember – resistance is futile". You smile at the desk clerk and follow the porter through the beautifully maintained historic home in the centre of Dunedin. On the landing, you turn away from the other differently themed rooms towards the Indian Suite. Soft music greets you as you enter another world, decorated with Indian motifs in lustrous shades of green, red, and gold. A solid brass elephant sits majestically in the room, offsetting the delicate antiquity of the writing desk and matching chairs. But it's not the large bed richly swathed in jewel bright fabrics that captures your attention. It's the cheeky smile on your partner's face, whose body lies beneath frothy bubbles in a black and gold claw footed bathtub situated a few feet from the bed.

AKA Resort Hua Hin | HUA HIN | THAILAND

Him: The footbridge leads to the candlelit pavilion. Lotus flowers float in the illuminated pond. The low teak table is set for an intimate dinner for two. Across another footbridge, the chef waits patiently with fresh ingredients and woks simmering on a low fire. The butler stands discretely to the side, chilling champagne in tall silver buckets. Tugging at his shirt, he swallows and pats his pocket for the umpteenth time to make sure that the little box is still there. He breaks out in a sweat, which is soon cooled by the tropical breeze. He hears the soft click, click of high heels, and thinks, this is it! Her: Opening the door to their exclusive villa at the AKA Resort, she is surprised by a trail of rose petals lit by flickering candles. On the four-poster bed she sees the note. Taking a deep breath she steps out on to the deck, following the petals and candlelight into the night...

Shiroganeya | KAGA | JAPAN

As the first light of the day dances over the serene garden outside, you raise the delicate cup to your lips. As the tea moves over your tongue you delight in its unique taste, then enjoy the warm sensation as you feel it move through your body. You imagine that this tea was one of the many reasons why Japan's highest ranking Samurai's enjoyed their rest and relaxation at Shiroganeya, and you marvel at the way the traditional Kaga style ryokan, uncompromisingly, integrates modern day comforts with the best of their traditions established over its 400 year history. Your desire to experience the wondrous hot springs at Shiroganeya takes you to the ryokan's open-air bath. As you immerse yourself in the warm silky waters, you smile to yourself and recall your Sensei's words in your final Japanese language class. The Sensei did say that immersion in Japanese culture is the best way to develop your language skills further.

Amankora | PARO | BHUTAN

Amankora offered a fantastic opportunity to experience a breathtaking country in a relatively short period of time. Both your pre-arranged guide and your driver took great care of the two of you from the minute you stepped off the plane in Paro until your departure. True to your adventurous nature, you visited all four Amankora lodges in Bhutan; spending two nights at Thimphu, one night at Gangtey, two nights at Punakha, and your last three nights at Amankora Paro. Just the right amount of time at each location - and finishing up with a visit to the Amankora spa was a superb suggestion. In fact, spending the final nights at Paro was ideal overall – it gave you a break from long car rides and avoided a long drive to the Paro airport when it was time to go home.

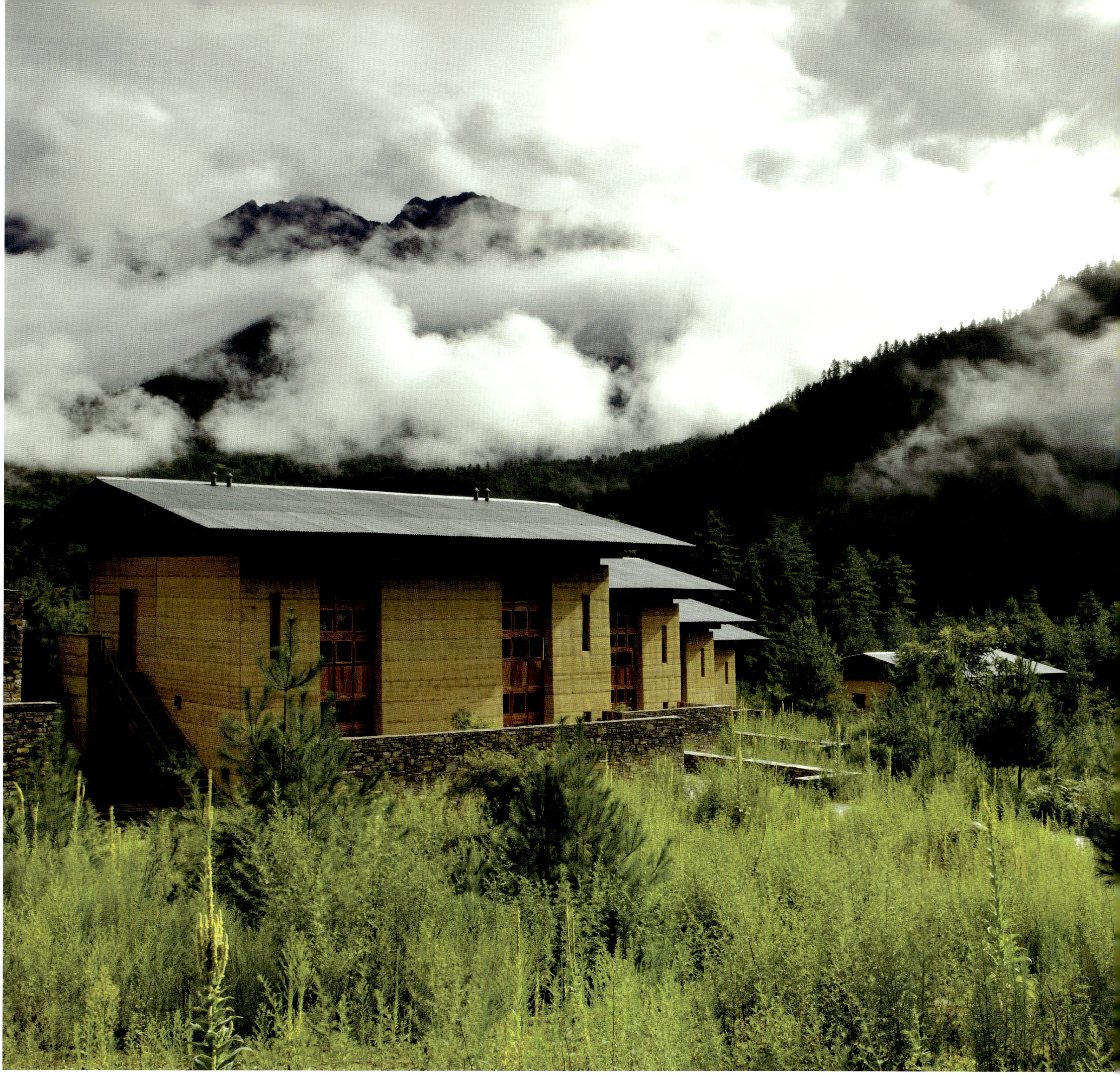

Lake Taupo Lodge | ACACIA BAY, NORTH ISLAND | NEW ZEALAND

While your wife and daughter are happy to spend the day lounging at the Lake Taupo Lodge, playing tennis and reading magazines, you are off for a long awaited chartered boat fishing expedition. Lake Taupo is reputed to be teeming with fat and feisty trout, so much so that your guide has already confidently told you that he will have you hooked up to a fish before day's end. And interestingly enough, your guide has also informed you that you can't actually buy trout in the restaurants of Taupo, but instead can bring your catch into many of the local restaurants and they will cook it for you! Now you are determined to catch at minimum three fish (since you will probably be expected to feed your wife and daughter too.)

Anantara Resort Hua Hin | HUA HIN | THAILAND

You had no idea that the Anantara Resort hosts the King's Cup Elephant Polo match every year, but you've arrived just in time for the annual event. They tell you it's like polo but with elephants. You wouldn't miss this for the world. In the meantime, you have several days to feel the cool breeze from the Gulf of Siam on your face; to swim beneath the shade of a fragrant Frangipani tree, to dine outdoors and listen to the sound of surf pounding in the background, to merge with nature in the tropical gardens surrounding this Thai sanctuary. Finally, the big day is here and you watch as two-ton elephants stampede across the field, waiting for their jockey's mallet to connect with the little white ball. The action thrills the crowds. The spectators stand on their feet clapping and cheering. Now if only the polo matches back home were as exciting.

Red Capital Ranch | THE GREAT WALL, MUNICIPALITY OF BEIJING | CHINA

There are some sights that are better than others to view on your own, and the Great Wall of China is one of them. On advice from a friend, you headed an hour outside Beijing to stay at the Red Capital Ranch. Set on a 50-acre private estate in a secluded valley surrounded by mountains, with rivers weaving throughout, the estate was really an old Manchurian hunting lodge completely surrounded by the infamous Great Wall. The food served at the hotel was organic and fresh cooked, and the wine list was great; but it was the 360-degree vista views of the Great Wall of China that made your stay such a pleasurable experience. From the hotel, you were able to hike on the Great Wall, by yourself, with no crowds or souvenir sellers to slow your step.

The Lodge at Paratiho Farms | NELSON, SOUTH ISLAND | NEW ZEALAND

You learned an important lesson: if paradise doesn't come to you, you must come to paradise. That is why you booked a one-week stay at New Zealand's "Paratiho" - the modern Maori word for paradise. As you roll up to the gates, you announce your arrival. Driving down the valley past rolling pastures of grazing sheep, deer, and cattle, you realise you're actually on a large 2000-acre working farm. It isn't until the main building appears in the midst of waterways and carefully manicured lawns that you realise that this is also a luxury lodge. Entering your suite, you see a lounge area with fireplace, a dressing nook, and enormous bathrooms with claw-foot tubs - all tastefully decorated in an eclectic mix of Asian and European influences. The large, airy room opens to lush gardens with beautiful sculptures, leaving no barrier between inside and out. You wonder if Adam and Eve ever had it this good.

Seiryuso | SHIMODA | JAPAN

You follow your partner along the flagstone path that leads to the Seiryuso traditional Japanese pavilion that is your own. Ancient willow trees guard your steps and lanterns offer glowing arcs to light your way. Reluctant to intrude on the serenity of the night, you softly whisper to one another as you reminisce about your delicious Casa Vino meal of sashimi with lobster, spring vegetables, and Moorish enochi mushroom fried rice. Reaching your rooms you quickly slip into matching bathrobes. Anticipation sizzles in the chilly night air as you step outside to the steaming outdoor bath that is fed from thermal springs. Cherry blossom trees, their limbs blooming with white and pink flowers that look like tiny snowflakes, stretch towards the midnight blue velvet of the night sky. Slipping into the warm mineral water - only the two of you in this winter paradise.

Burrawang West Station | BURRAWANG, NEW SOUTH WALES | AUSTRALIA

Okay, so some restructuring was in order. A number of employees were let go. A few VPs received packages. Senior staff's been restless since, so it's time for some team bonding. This kind of rebuilding requires space and time, and there's nowhere better than Burrawang West Station, where everyone can spread out across 10,000 acres of country in Central New South Wales and, hopefully, end up reconnecting as a team. Some head off on bikes. Others golf. You take time to fish the Lachlan River, wondering if, by day's end, everyone will be holed up in private rooms. (You can't blame them. A scotch by your room's fireplace is starting to look pretty nice.) Instead, when you return, there are steaks on the barbecue and all your staff are lounging outside, enjoying themselves. Perhaps even bonding. The fireplace can wait. You pull up a chair.

Peppers Spicers Peak Lodge | MARYVALE, QUEENSLAND | AUSTRALIA

Yesterday was two wheels; today it's four. The mountain bikes were a challenge to be sure – actually, not so much the bikes as the terrain. They call this high country wilderness, which is fine when you're up there, but after taking the somewhat easy route 'down', the 'up' parts weren't quite so much fun. "But the challenge is half the fun!" "Yes, dear, that's right (grumble, grumble)." At least today's four wheel driving tour of the national park isn't as hard on the old ticker – it's just all the jarring and bumping over rough terrain that keeps reminding you so vividly of every single muscle you stressed yesterday. But relief is on the way. The next two days at Peppers Spicers Peak Lodge will be all about your scheduled activities – nothing at all, followed by nothing at all, then after a late afternoon massage, more of nothing at all.

Uma Paro | PARO | BHUTAN

You were not sure what to expect in Bhutan but it definitely wasn't the Uma Paro. You've stayed in a lot of nice hotels over the years, but the Uma Paro far exceeded all of them. The staff was extremely friendly, immensely helpful, and thoroughly accommodating. You arranged the details of your trip through the hotel and, upon arrival, you were assigned a guide and a driver; both were fabulous. Your guide not only knew everything about the history, the flora and fauna, the culture, the religion, and the landmarks, he also was very helpful when you couldn't figure out how to use your new camera. The hikes you did were strenuous but worth the effort as the sites were unparalleled - monasteries seemingly growing out of the rocks, an unbelievable waterfall, a 16th century watch tower, not to mention the extensive view of villages and farmlands below.

The Empire Hotel & Country Club | BORNEO | BRUNEI DARRUSSALAM

You have traveled through Brunei to other Asian cities as well as to Europe on several occasions, but this time you and your wife have arranged for a full weeks stay. As always, you will be staying at The Empire Hotel & Country Club, as you have regularly found the accommodation, including the "E Club", to be first rate - comfortable, clean, and with all the amenities one would expect from a Five Star Plus establishment. The beds are "heavenly" and all king-sized. Dining in the Atrium Cafe is an experience you are confident your wife will enjoy every bit as much as you have in the past. Fresh seafood from Australia, smoked salmon from Scotland, and Asian dishes are to die for; not to mention a good selection of European dishes to choose from, including top quality steaks.

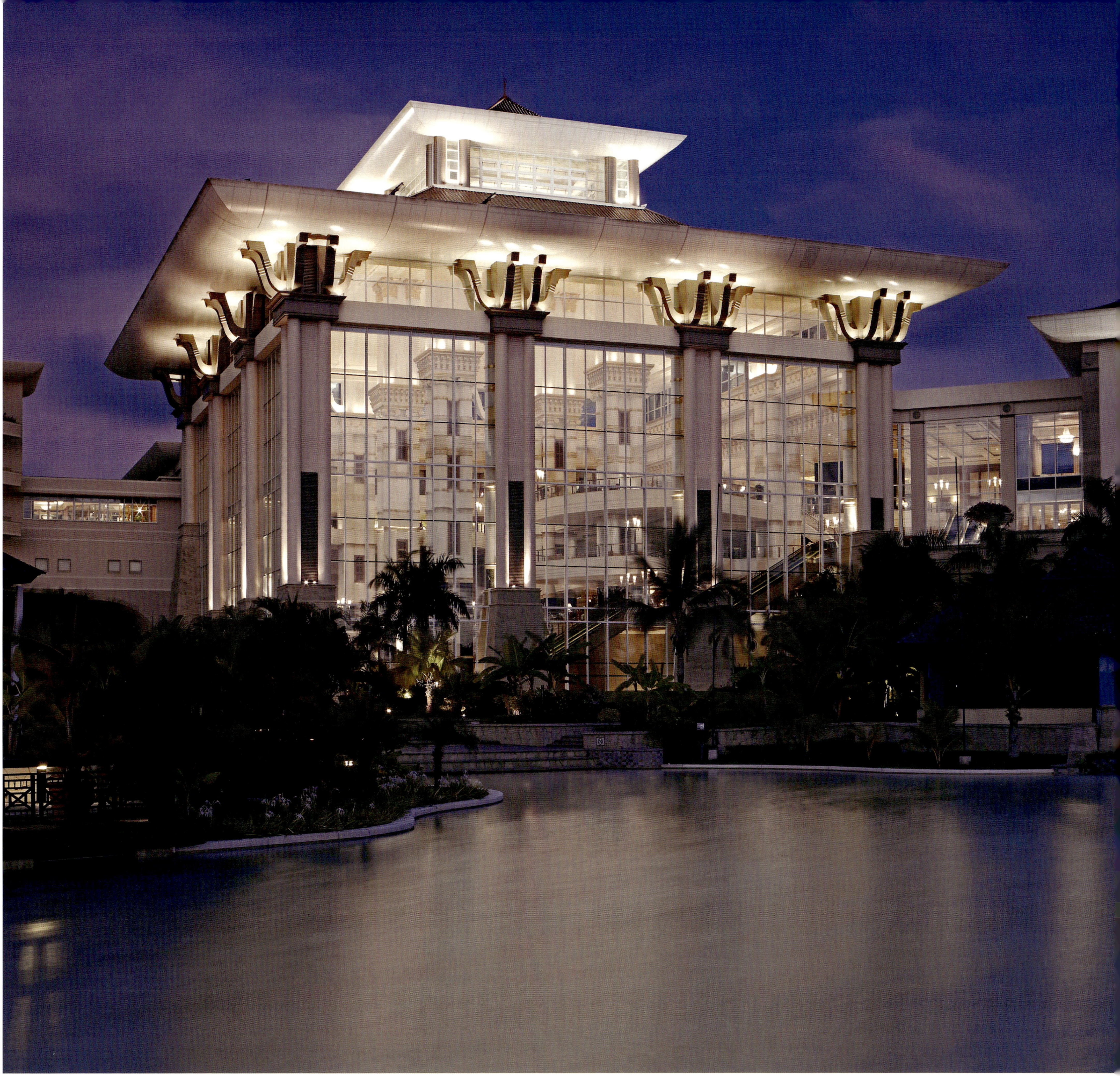

Fuchun Resort | HANGZHOU, ZHEJIANG PROVINCE | CHINA

Your parents owned a Chinese print by Yuan Dynasty painter, Huang Gongwang: an image of a landscape in which man and nature become one. When your parents died, the print was forgotten, your family neglected. Then your sister reappeared in your life. Thrilled to see her, you propose a trip. Her choice. "Alright," she says, "but it's somewhere you've been before." You fly to Hangzhou, in the Zhejiang Province of China. She's wrong – you've never visited this region, but you're happy to have arrived. The Fuchun Resort is astonishingly beautiful, set in a traditional Chinese landscape with picturesque villages, mountain ranges, and a tea plantation. Yoga, tai chi, golf, and other pleasures are available for the taking. Suddenly, walking through the grounds, you stop. You have been here before. This area was the inspiration for Gongwang's art, for the print from your childhood. Memories flood your mind. Gratefully, you thank your sis. Turns out she was right, after all.

KIWICOLLECTION.COM

Black Barn Vineyards | HAVELOCK NORTH, NORTH ISLAND | NEW ZEALAND

A morning 'lie-in' for both you and your partner. Then a mid-morning expedition with the whole family to the market and an early lunch, at the Black Barn Bistro, that satisfies everyone's fresh air inspired hearty appetites. Followed by a giggling fruit stained afternoon of picking figs in the vineyard's orchards for dessert. At the end of the day, your partner leads you out to the terrace of your lodge, leaving your rambunctious teenagers at the breakfast bench devouring the last of their figs and ice cream. The chardonnay is a muted gold as you raise your glass in an unspoken toast to the slopes of Te Mata Peak and the Tuki Tuki River that chuckles and dances past the lodge. A slam of the front door and the children have departed for the concert to be held at the vineyard's amphitheatre. A wink from your partner and you both realise the kids will be gone for hours.

The Lalu, Sun Moon Lake | YUCHR SHIANG NANTOU | TAIWAN

You arrived at The Lalu, Sun Moon Lake in Taiwan the day before Chinese New Year, with your husband and three children, a little unsure of what to expect. Travelling with the children is always a gamble; their wants and tastes being so different from your own. Fortunately, your husband had booked a two-bedroom villa that offered a gorgeous lake view (by which you could take the time to read and relax) and, even better, a private heated pool that promised to supply hours of entertainment for the excited children. To your surprise, the pool ended up providing hours of entertainment for you and your husband as well. With the pool heated to 29 degrees swimming at night was just as pleasant as it was during the day, and proved a very relaxing and rejuvenating way to end each evening, especially after the day's mayhem of Chinese New Year activities.

Quay West Resort, Bunker Bay | BUNKER BAY, WESTERN AUSTRALIA | AUSTRALIA

Some might suggest August is not the most hospitable time of year to visit Margaret River – weather wise, that is. But this all depends on where you stay. Fortunately you stayed at the Quay West Resort, Bunker Bay, which happens to be well suited to all types of weather. The large airy rooms, that are so obviously wonderful during summer, are well heated and cosy during cooler climes. The main building, with its great deck and stunning views of Bunker Bay, is an ideal spot for breakfast or a glass of wine in the sun. And when it is cooler, the open fireplace offers an inviting location to congregate and read papers or books. Of course, the highlight of the stay was actually the spa – something that actually can be enjoyed more in bad weather than in good.

Delamore Lodge | WAIHEKE ISLAND, NORTH ISLAND | NEW ZEALAND

In the speech last night they said you had always been the envy of your friends. As you sit in bed watching the sun rise over the deep blue waters of the Hauraki Gulf, whether that was an exaggeration or not, at this moment, it certainly feels as if it could be true. It pleases you to think that your closest friends are also sharing this breathtaking view from the other three suites. It's your birthday that has brought all of you together at Delamore Lodge. You surprised them with a helicopter that arrived to take you all directly to the lodge. They surprised you with a private chef and an exquisite dinner of fresh seafood from the bay, enjoyed with local wines from the lodge's wine cellar. You smile as you recall some of last night's conversation – which of you was going to win tomorrow's round of golf? You reminded them that it was your birthday, after all.

KIWICOLLECTION.COM

Moonlight Head Private Lodge | YUULONG, VICTORIA | AUSTRALIA

You've been home for a month, but you still haven't come down to earth. You go through your day as if in a trance. The rituals of life are somehow less vivid and real than your time at Moonlight Head Private Lodge. You remember walking for hours, discovering new coves, waterfalls, and views of the Great Southern Ocean. You smile at the memory of all those lambs and sheep frolicking on the 1500-acre private farm; the free-range wildlife sanctuary where you spied rare species of kangaroos, wallabies, echidnas, and koalas. Waking up in a plush duvet bed with views of the startling coast, you felt the other world of city noise and errands receding into the background. You never expected to get so attached to this place; to the peaceful serenity of a completely disconnected world.

Wharekauhau | WAIRARAPA, NORTH ISLAND | NEW ZEALAND

When Grandfather started the family business, this was his motto: Make it the best, and make it real. In taking over the helm, you've tried to live up to his standards, but you wonder if you've lost the original vision. Are you doing the right thing with the business? Making the best decisions? Most of all, would he be proud? It's all too overwhelming, enough for you to want to escape to the middle of nowhere. A place like Wharekauhau, a rural retreat on New Zealand's North Island. A room with a king-sized four-poster bed, vintage wines every night. The Rimutaka Ranges to the west, Palliser Bay to the east, with a sheep station that's been in operation for over 150 years. Here everything is the best and, what's more, there's not a touch of artificiality anywhere. Much, you realise, like the way you run the family business. Yes, Grandfather would be proud.

Ceylon Tea Trails | HATTON | SRI LANKA

The debate around the family dinner table was getting more lively by the minute. Which of the four painstakingly restored British tea merchants' houses would be your home for the holidays? Was it to be the country cottage appeal of Summerville, the eclectic style of Castlereagh, the whimsical 60's styling of Norwood, or the colonial splendour of Tientsin. It seemed nobody could agree. Some wanted to be near the lake while others wanted to be up on the hillside. Your family was at an impasse and was now looking at you to end the stalemate. Clearing your throat, you looked sternly across the table and declared that the only solution was to extend your holiday by a week and split your time between two – Summerville by the lake and the one up on the hillside with the pool, Norwood. And with that definitive declaration the dinner table debate was transformed, instantly, into squeals of delight.

Ruffles Lodge | GOLD COAST, QUEENSLAND | AUSTRALIA

The ground falls away beneath you as you fly like an eagle over the Gold Coast hinterland. In the distance, the deep aqua of the Pacific Ocean is bordered by golden sand. Below you, the tropical rainforest is broken by bushwalking treks and shimmering cascades and waterfalls fed by natural springs. An inquisitive cockatoo hovers above the wing of your hang glider - a friendly companion - before catching the slipstream and soaring off towards the clouds. As the glider turns in a lazy circle, you swoop lower. Your partner waves cheerfully from the landing site. What is it about Ruffles Lodge that is so exceptional? Perhaps it's the familiar welcome you received from your hosts on arrival, or the appetising dinner of locally grown and sourced produce. Your feet skid to a stop as you touch down. Looking into your partner's smiling face, you realise it's about being able to enjoy it all with that special someone.

Gora Kadan | KANAGAWA | JAPAN

The raindrops splashing into the hot springs surrounding your Kadan Suite ring out with the chime of fine crystal. As you stand in the doorway overlooking your private garden, a giant granite Jacuzzi tub beckons you outside. There is a gentle stream cascading through the garden that keeps your tub filled to overflowing with warm mineral-rich spring water. Lush green leaves of Japanese pine and bamboo envelop dark grey granite slabs that separate you from the other guests. And, although you know you are in complete privacy, you still look sheepishly to the left and right before slipping off your wooden clogs, split toed socks, and traditional cotton robe. The gentle mist mixed with the steam rising from the tub tickles your skin and sends a tingle down your spine. The experience of standing nude in your private enclave is exhilarating and you pause for an extra moment before giving in to your modesty and slipping into the tub.

Lake Okareka Lodge | ROTORUA, NORTH ISLAND | NEW ZEALAND

The seaplane gives a jaunty wave of its wings before disappearing over the surrounding mountains, abandoning you. Dusk falls on Lake Okareka Lodge; it's just you, the rainbow trout, and your favourite lure and fly-fishing reel. Oh, and your partner, of course. The crackle of the barbeque and the smell of roasting potatoes tease your nostrils as you contemplate the dark waters of the lake. There, lurking just below the surface, is a cunning, mischievous, record sized trout and you are determined to land him this year. You refuse to return home empty handed. Turning from the lake, you content yourself with an expedition of a different nature, to the extremely well stocked wine cellar and to the library where a vast array of books await your perusal. Watching your partner tend the barbeque, you realise that everything you need to make this getaway perfect is right here, at the lodge.

Thorngrove Manor Hotel | ADELAIDE, SOUTH AUSTRALIA | AUSTRALIA

Candlelight, glinting off the antique sterling silver cutlery, flickers invitingly from the linen topped table. Mr D. - Entering the room he voices his apologies for his unavoidably late arrival to the dining party. As he takes his seat, his attention is captured by sparkling eyes across the table. In a fog, he rises with the other gentlemen to relocate by the fire as the butler relays the table for dessert. Miss E.B.- Since arriving at the Manor she has felt flung back in time, to an era of leafy country lanes and baroque coaches drawn by matching horses, all set within the reality of the Adelaide Hills. As promised by her host, her room is a romantic European whimsy. Heart beating quickly, she chances a surreptitious glance at the handsome stranger. Butler - The guests resume their seats. As he serves the delicate concoction of frozen berries and pannacotta, he's not surprised to discover that Mr D. has relocated to the seat beside Miss E.B.

Banyan Tree Ringha | TIBET, YUNNAN PROVINCE | CHINA

Banyan Tree Ringha is not your typical Banyan Tree experience. If you're expecting swimming pools, golf courses, tennis courts, and the like, you are in for a surprise. A word of advice: don't take your Gucci shoes and pin stripe suit; trade them in for a nice, warm fleece jacket and practical hiking boots. Located in an amazingly serene, calm, and remote area of Yunnan, your accommodation at the Banyan Tree Ringha is in a rustic, and secluded, Tibetan farmhouse surrounded by lakes and valleys. The pigs, goats, and yaks are actually quite adorable. And if altitude sickness is a concern, and let's face it, at 3200 metres above sea level, it's certainly something to think about; fear not, there are endless cups of ginger tea for your pleasure, and the tour guides and hotel staff are always equipped with oxygen bottles (just in case).

Lilianfels Blue Mountains | KATOOMBA, NEW SOUTH WALES | AUSTRALIA

Pushing back the duvet, I follow the scent of freshly brewed coffee across the room. I sit on the arm of my spouse's chair. "It's a beautiful morning here at Lilianfels." I have to agree, "Yes, it is." I can smell the eucalyptus and wattle trees that are abundant here in the Blue Mountains. Gazing through the window, I watch as the crimson rosellas and cockatoos native to this area play tag in the trees. "What would you like to do today? There's bushwalking, the Scenic Railway, or, a picnic in the National Park?" "Hmmm. A picnic sounds good. But maybe we should order in." I pointedly look from my spouse to the oversized bed of inviting white and cream linen and back to my spouse. "The deep canyons and the waterfalls of the Jamison Valley have been here for thousands of years." Chuckling, my spouse reaches for me. "Happy 45th anniversary, my darling!"

KIWICOLLECTION.COM

Tower Lodge | POKOLBIN, NEW SOUTH WALES | AUSTRALIA

You'll discover that the Tower Lodge on the Tower Estate Winery is like a fine bottle of aged Hunter Valley wine. The Lodge is resplendent beneath the golden sunshine, similar to a buttery oaked Chardonnay. It also possesses the palatable qualities of a big Shiraz; bursting with hidden surprises and richer elements of luxurious comfort, topped with a peppery finish. Like the fabulous wine of the region, the Lodge is a well-balanced, smooth, and rounded getaway for any aspiring wine connoisseur. Don't forget your golf clubs; The Dinks 18-hole golf course is at your doorstep. Remember to leave the bicycles behind and take the horse-drawn carriage on your tour of the vineyards. You'll be grateful for the bench seat, after all those tastings, and for the extra space to hold those cases of your favourite vintages.

Huka Lodge | TAUPO, NORTH ISLAND | NEW ZEALAND

As you soak in one of the hot pools at Huka Lodge, you listen to the haunting voice of Dame Kiri te Kanawa echoeing in the breathtaking vista of mountain peaks and rushing waters of the Waikato River. A few more moments and you will retire to your room to dress before meeting your friends in the main Lodge Room. There, a blazing fire and pre-dinner aperitifs await you and your fellow guests. No doubt, tonight's discussion will involve tall tales of even taller fish. This evening, you are prepared and possess strong digital evidence to support your claim to fly-fishing supremacy. You are confidant that you landed a record sized brown trout this afternoon on Lake Taupo. Fortunately, you managed to capture it on your digital camera, just before the crafty trout slipped the lure and slid beneath the chill crystal waters of the lake. Naturally, you'll be back on the lake tomorrow to determine who's the more intelligent, you or the trout.

COUNTRYSIDE 93

Wildflower Hall | SHIMLA, HIMACHAL PRADESH | INDIA

At 8,500 feet, the air filling your lungs feels unmistakably crisp and clean. Not cold, by any means, but invigorating and rejuvenating. The soothing sound of your Yogi's voice, without judgment or criticism, guides your movements. Focus on your breathing, she reminds you. Fill your belly, your chest, and your throat with air. She encourages you to exhale fully and assures you that, with each breath, you are releasing tension and stress. You never could have imagined that the simple act of breathing could require so much attention and result in such deep relaxation. Now, perched high above the giant cedar forests of this spectacular Himalayan hideaway, your mind has been temporarily released from the rigors of measuring margins, profits, and return on investment. And you are free, if only for a few days, to focus fully on your own personal health and well-being. Arguably the best investment you have made this year.

The Lodge at Tarraleah | TARRALEAH, TASMANIA | AUSTRALIA

They said it was a relaxing and peaceful activity – trout fishing. Sounded good at the time. And, if you were going to try your hand at it, what better place than here in the highlands of Tasmania, with a guide from The Lodge at Tarraleah. What they neglected to mention was all the hiking, climbing, trudging, stream fording, unstable ground-walking on… and all those myriad of other little things that have left you exhausted, albeit enthralled with your new-found sport (no complaining about sore arms from reeling in all those catches!). Now with a glass of fine wine in hand, you're enjoying what you define as the 'relaxing and peaceful' portion of the day's activity – a long and luxurious soak in the cliff top hot tub, overlooking the amazing view from the lodge.

KIWICOLLECTION.COM

Grasmere Lodge High Country Retreat | CASS, SOUTH ISLAND | NEW ZEALAND

You came to New Zealand looking for excitement. After all, this is the country that invented the inboard jet engine, bungee jumping, and zorbing. But after weeks of touring, you found out that the natural beauty of New Zealand is all the excitement you need; which is why you checked into Grasmere Lodge High Country Retreat to spend some time alone. With the lodge spread out over acres of lush mountain land, your cottage is five minutes from the main lodge. You worry about feeling isolated. So you sign up for horse riding. Riding through rich native forests, waterfalls, alpine herb gardens, and mountaintops; and breathing the air of the Southern Alps - nothing could be better than this. You wonder if you're becoming too much of a lone ranger. But then you get the call. Drinks and hors d' oeuvres at 7:30 PM. Dinner at 8 PM sharp. You were planning to dine alone on your terrace, but accept the invitation. As you step into the dining room, you are greeted by smiling faces of the owners and guests. Instantly, you feel welcome and at home. Tomorrow, there will be plenty of time to be alone.

The River House | BALAPITIYA | SRI LANKA

There is "fresh" seafood, and then there is "fresh" seafood that is caught and prepared in the same day, sometimes within several hours. And, that is what you are enjoying at this very moment. A plate full of juicy jumbo prawns plucked from the ocean not far from where you are sitting with a glass of champagne in your hand and sun baked sand between your toes. Earlier in the day, you declined an invitation to try your luck with rod and reel and chose, instead, to try surfing in Hikkaduwa – a world-renowned surf town just around the corner. Packed with backpackers, hippies, and surf gods, that charming little town reminded you of your days as an intrepid traveller with nothing more than a backpack and a pair of flip flops. Fond memories, indeed. But nothing you would trade for the memories you are making at this very moment.

COUNTRYSIDE

Eichardt's Private Hotel | QUEENSTOWN, SOUTH ISLAND | NEW ZEALAND

Following in the footsteps of the outrageous rogues and alpine explorers of Queenstown's past, you sit before the roaring fire in The Parlour at Eichardt's sipping your fragrant brew of choice. Like the eccentric characters of the gold mining days you procrastinate, lingering in the understated luxury of the hotel, listening to the interesting anecdotes of your fellow guests. Your journal lies open on the side table, its pages invitingly blank. The discussion turns to dinner and to the wealth of first-class culinary establishments only a short walk from the hotel. Good-natured debate ensues, eloquent voices raised in praise for the variety of local produce sourced from the wild waters of the ocean and the verdant pastures of the countryside. A challenge is issued. Everyone is invited to decide for himself. As you look into the fire you realise you are not ready to move just yet.

Taj Lake Palace | UDAIPUR, RAJASTHAN | INDIA

Holding the diamond up to the sun you are captivated by its brilliance. The gentle rocking of the boat delivers you back to reality and you suddenly realise that you are dwarfed by the grand white marbled facade of the Taj Lake Palace. You have never seen such a strikingly beautiful interior; the decorative paintwork and ornate architecture a welcome distraction from the butterflies in your stomach. Through the marble pillars you catch a glimpse of the Lily Pond. Its fairytale ambiance confirms that it is perfect for tonight. You enter your suite and lay on the bed, the diamond ring in your pocket pressing into your leg. Nervous energy gets you up and you walk out to your private balcony. The view across the lake to the Aravalli Mountains and Jagmandir Palace is truly awe-inspiring. Now you have two important questions - where is the perfect place to propose? The other goes without saying.

Mandarin Oriental Dhara Dhevi, Chiang Mai | CHIANG MAI | THAILAND
Dispersed among the historically accurate architecture of this resort's 60 palatial acres are four world-class restaurants. So the question is, where do you dine tonight? Relishing the thought of such a delicious decision, you let your mind return to last night's supper at Farang Ses: exceptional French cuisine that would surely satisfy the most particular Parisian. The night before: Thai food at Le Grande Lanna. Designed as a replica of a Lanna Nobleman's home, their menu is regarded by Thailand's most discerning to be one of the best. Dim sum at The Mandarin Oriental lived up to its reputation… but that was lunch today. That leaves the continental delights of Akaligo for this evening. Good, that settles that. Now, of the three stunningly beautiful bars, where will you enjoy an aperitif?

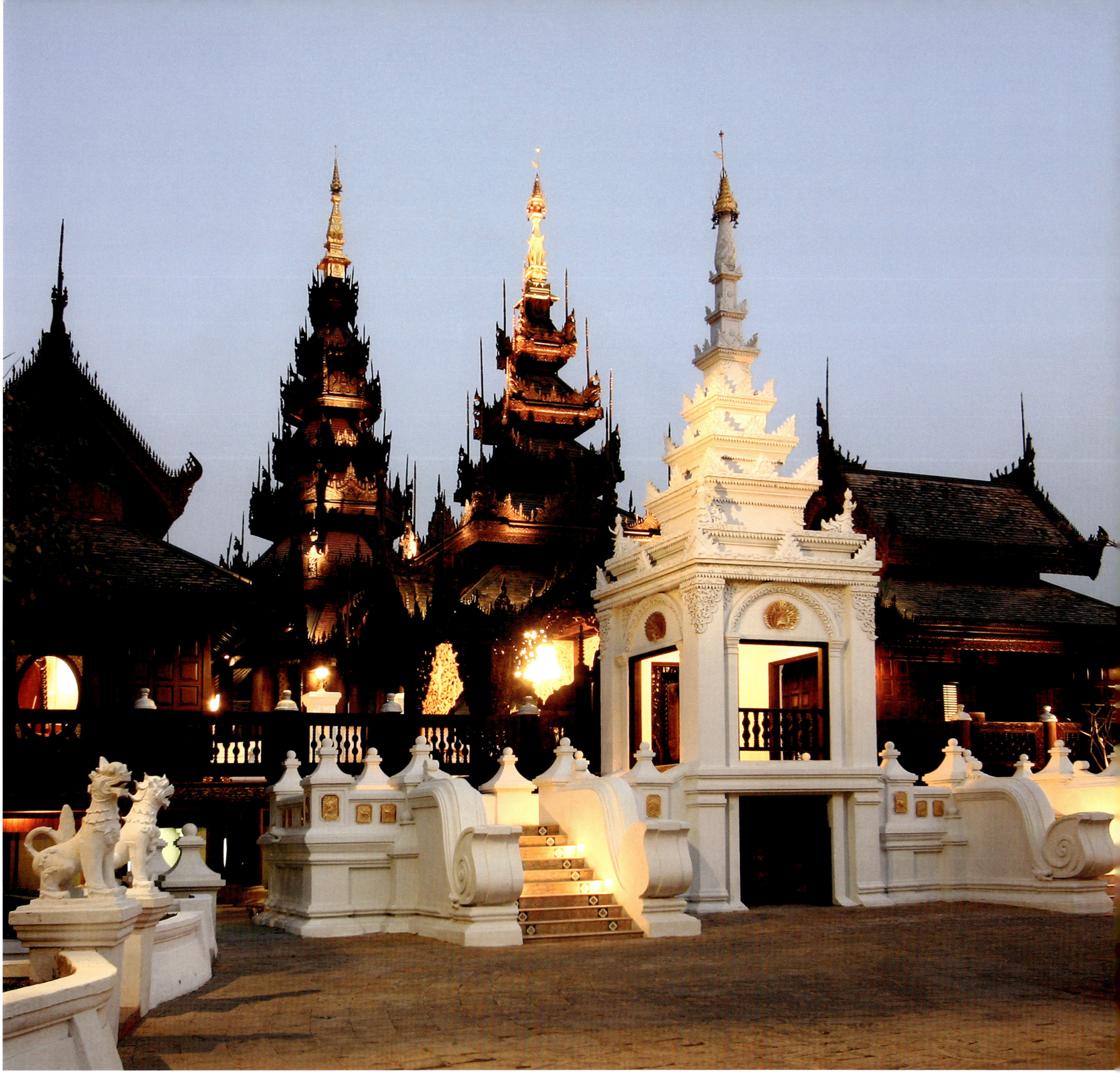

Whare Kea Chalet | WANAKA, SOUTH ISLAND | NEW ZEALAND

The Whare Kea Chalet, situated high in New Zealand's Southern Alps, certainly was not the simplest place in the world to reach, but you have recently come to realise that some of the best of treasures are well hidden and not easily accessible. That is, after all, what makes them "treasures". The helicopter transport right to the front lawn of the resort was smooth enough, and made for a grand and awe-inspiring arrival. The Chalet itself was a hidden gem, surprisingly secluded yet adorned with all the modern amenities you expect from a luxury accommodation. And after settling into your room you happily accepted a glass of champagne before dinner. Best to rest up tonight, as the days ahead will be filled with exhausting, but exhilarating alpine walks high into the scenic mountains.

Gyalthang Dzong Hotel | TIBET, YUNNAN PROVINCE | CHINA

Travelling is about adventure: discovering new sights and sounds, experiencing different cultures, and, of course, trying new things. And your recent stay at Gyalthang Dzong Hotel is certainly no exception. Housed in a Tibetan lamasery style building located in the south eastern end of the Tibetan Plateau, you know immediately this is not going to be your typical resort vacation. Resplendent with nature walks through limestone and granite terrain and visits to ancient Tibetan monasteries, the week promises to hold many new and exciting adventures. And somewhere along the way you have vowed to try yet one more new thing – the famous yak steak at the hotel's restaurant, reported to be very good. (And no, it doesn't taste like chicken.)

Bulgari Hotels & Resorts, Bali | ULUWATU, BALI | INDONESIA
Secreted away to a mysterious fortress, hidden behind volcanic walls and shrouded in lush tropical plants perched on a cliff top, you couldn't imagine what to expect. From the moment you arrived and were given the menu of hotel services by your butler, you have been astounded and delighted by the personalised care you have received. Now you rest your chin on your hands, as you lay on the massage table beside the infinity edge pool that appears to plunge off the cliffs edge to the shore below. Before you, the view stretches towards the horizon; white sandy beaches and frothy waves that dance on the edge of the endless aqua waters of the Indian Ocean. You dissolve as the therapist places hot lava stones along your back in a traditional Balinese healing ritual. You cannot wait to be whisked back to Bulgari Hotels & Resorts, Bali again next year.

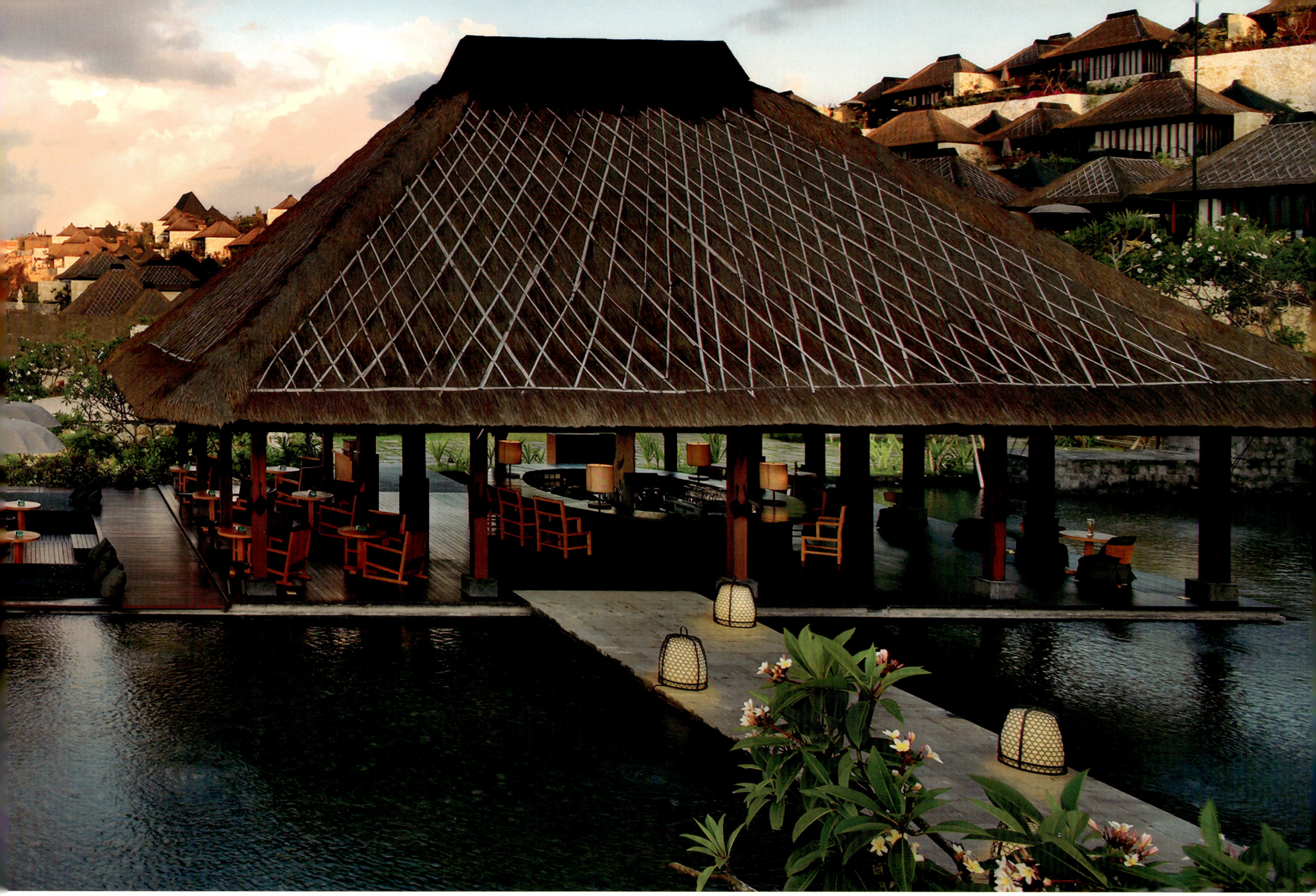

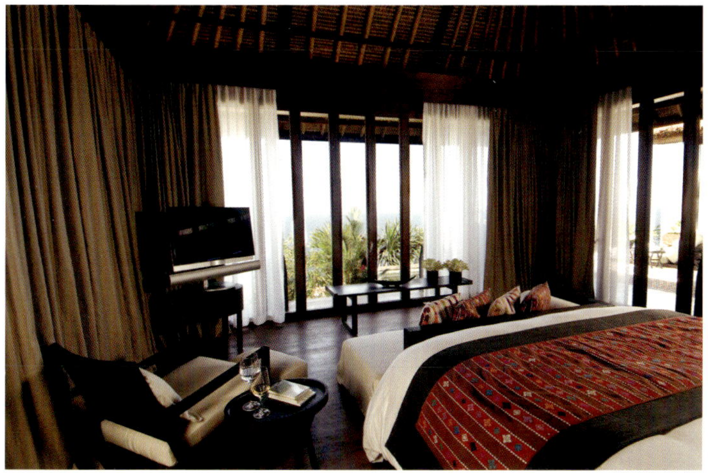

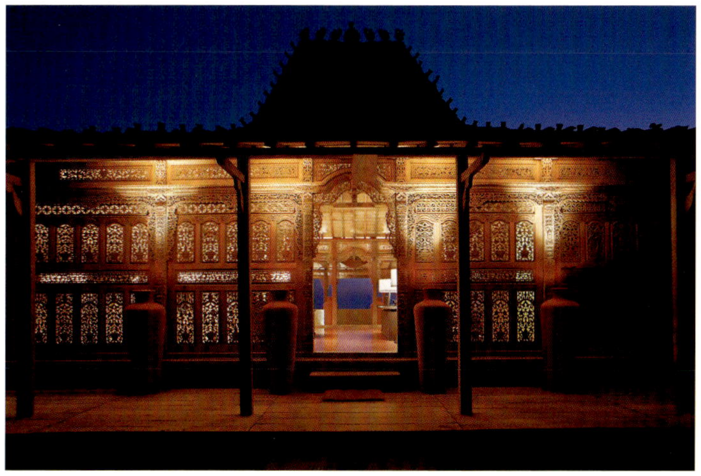

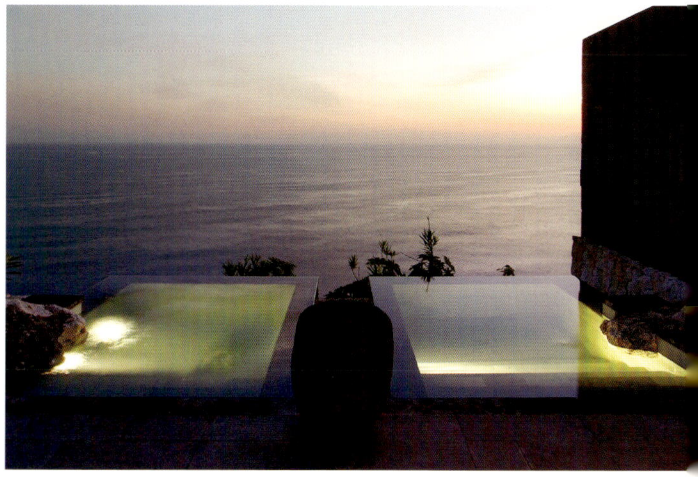

Gaia Retreat & Spa | BYRON BAY, NEW SOUTH WALES | AUSTRALIA

The current pace of your life has not been without reward, but it has begun to take its toll on your body, mind, and spirit. However, as you lay quietly in the fresh lemongrass and mint bath, you realise that the tension that has built up in your shoulders over the last year has no chance against the skilled hands of the masseuse waiting in the next room. Moving from the tub to the massage table, you are treated to an all-over body butter massage that relaxes you body while invigorating your senses with essential oils of ginger and lime. The motion of the therapist's hands begins to free your mind from thoughts of men in boring suits and of your diligent, but omnipresent, assistant. Hmmm… If she could only see you now, what would she say? Something about a deadline you missed, no doubt. On second thought, perhaps it's best she can't see you now.

The Rachamankha | CHIANG MAI | THAILAND

Indulgent pleasures and meaningful pursuits will be your reward. But, first, you must switch off your mobile phone and leave the exciting bustle of Chiang Mai behind. Step into a world created with love and a faithful attention to detail: this is The Rachamankha, a treasure chest overflowing with Chinese antiquities and Lanna art. From the moment you step inside the cool interiors, you feel the pressures of life slip away and the peaceful serenity of your surroundings seep deep into your soul. The hotel's design, inspired by one of Thailand's most beautiful temples, soothes you with every step you take. As you join your work colleagues in the restaurant for another gourmet delight, you hope this team weekend of recuperation doesn't leave you too relaxed to tackle business on Monday.

Eagles Nest | RUSSELL, NORTH ISLAND | NEW ZEALAND

The champagne flute in your hand feels especially cold, particularly in comparison to the hot water flowing down your back. Until about five minutes ago, you had always considered the act of bathing to be a somewhat utilitarian activity. But now, standing beneath this cascade of steaming hot water, sipping Verve Clicquot, and taking in the breathtaking view of New Zealand's Bay of Islands, it appears you've been remiss in your earlier assessments. Of course, this is no ordinary shower. It is a totally private and sumptuous floor-to-ceiling glass enclosure that compliments the "glassed roof" design of your luxurious three-bedroom villa. And while you've always taken great pleasure in the artful combination of a beautiful vista and a delightful glass of bubbly, from this point forward you'll make an effort to incorporate your new-found appreciation for bathing into the mix.

KIWICOLLECTION.COM

Amanusa | NUSA DUA, BALI | INDONESIA

Weddings are not your favourite activity. This one takes place at dusk, so there are only fourteen hours until it's time to hop on the plane and go home. However, once the ceremony is over, you relax a bit on Amanusa's white sand beach; admire the expanse of the Indian Ocean at sunset, breathe in the scent of tuberoses. A friend of the groom's - correction, an attractive friend of the groom's - silently admires the view of Mount Agung. "God, I hate weddings", this person says. Excusing yourself, you locate a fresh bottle of champagne, return to the friend, and pour two glasses. The ocean has turned a deep blue, the setting sun lighting the tips of the water in tones of yellow and pink. Alas, a precious twelve hours until you have to go home. So little time. "To weddings", you say, holding up a filled glass. To weddings.

Lake House | DAYLESFORD, VICTORIA | AUSTRALIA

You are tempted to linger, admiring the view over the foreshore of Lake Daylesford from the luxurious comfort of your suite. However, the promise of something illusive whispers on the breeze, calling you to the Lake House's exceptional wellness retreat at the Salus Spa. Your partner may slog it out on the tennis court and commune with nature along the various bushwalks, but you enthusiastically will embark on a journey of self-discovery. Soak away your tension in the mineral water tubs. Allow the fresh air to recharge you from the inside out. Detox and energise your body with tasty meals of the locally grown organic produce. Several days later, you'll smile blissfully when your partner joins you, flushed with exertion, and bragging about that match-winning volley. Today, you achieved an inner harmony and balance in your life. Contentment.

The Oberoi Rajvilas, Jaipur | JAIPUR, RAJASTHAN | INDIA

This morning a mythical elephant safari to Naila Fort, this afternoon a retreat to meditative seclusion. You have turned the pages of history and stepped back in time. You have journeyed to this elegant oasis in the Rajasthani countryside. Here, the buildings are illuminated from within with the glowing pink of an autumn sunset and set against the dramatic backdrop of the desert sky. Like the mysterious Rajput Princes of history you indulge all your senses, allowing the decadent luxury of your surroundings at The Oberoi Rajvilas to rejuvenate and restore you. The water is cool on your fingertips as you run your hand along the reflection pool. The water ripples and, in the pink tinted reflection of the desert sky, you see the shadow of Rajas and noblewomen in bright saris gathered in celebration. Another ripple of the water and the image is gone.

Merribrook Retreat | MARGARET RIVER, WESTERN AUSTRALIA | AUSTRALIA

Figs freshly picked from the orchard are ripe and ready to be devoured. Chocolate banana bread, still warm from the oven, promises a hidden surprise of apricots. Kookaburras laugh uproariously from the eucalyptus trees at the wild fowl pecking their way across the rolling lawn to the lakes edge. As you follow the path from your secluded bush retreat at Merribrook Retreat, to the main lodge, you almost break into a jog in your eagerness to be the first to sample breakfast. You can smell the spinach and feta omelette browning in its pan in anticipation of your arrival. Perhaps this morning you will begin with the homemade muesli and fresh fruit, another step towards better health and well-being. Yesterday's quiet contemplation, by the lake, of your native surroundings relaxed and helped you to achieve an inner balance. Today you are ready to revitalise your spirit with an unforgettable adventure, abseiling down the Cape's oldest granite rocks. But first, breakfast, yum!

Aman-i-Khás | RANTHAMBHORE, RAJASTHAN | INDIA

Heart beating wildly, your book falls unnoticed from your fingers. Thoughts race through your mind as you blink and re-focus. The sound of the wind rustling through the grass of the savannah seems loud in your ears. As you stand in the opening to your opulent white tent, you realise that this was not what you had expected. The shadowed cool interior, the magnificent daybed, the indulgent soaking tub, and the king-sized bed all combine to conjure up an image of Maharajahs and times gone by. A flicker of movement, a switch of a long stripey tail, and you are held mesmerised beneath the setting sun. In the distance, the tiger stretches and shakes its head, its deep somber eyes watchful. With a flash of white teeth and a throaty chuckle, the feline turns and lopes off into the tall grass. You release the breath you've been holding. Uncle was right. Coming to Aman-i-Khás is more than just a luxurious break; it is a journey of discovery into a forgotten world.

Solitaire Lodge | ROTORUA, NORTH ISLAND | NEW ZEALAND

The delectable aroma of freshly caught rainbow trout grilling on a bed of tarragon and thyme wafts from the open kitchen. The chefs at Solitaire Lodge add a clove of garlic from the herb garden and a sprinkle of celery salt to the roasting locally grown vegetables, enhancing rather than overwhelming the natural flavours of the seasonal produce. Naturally, you would only trust the best of chefs to prepare your record size bounty landed fresh that day from the deck of the luxury catamaran on Lake Tarawera. Exhilarated after a day spent fishing for wily trout on crystal waters, you sip your glass of chilled Sauvignon Blanc. The light floral tones swirl around your mouth leaving a hint of honey and passion fruit to tease your palate. Shortly, you will be summoned to join your fellow guests at the lodge in the comfortable dining room for yet another culinary celebration.

Baghvan | PENCH NATIONAL PARK, RAJASTHAN | INDIA

During your stay in the magnificently comfortable atmosphere of the old forest rest houses at Baghvan, you plan to take a day to visit and explore India's famous Pench National Park, a 118 square mile sanctuary and tiger reserve. The undulating terrain of the Pench National Park is a bamboo jungle of small hills and is reputed to be well-stocked with Indian Teak. According to your guide Cheeta, SamBAR and Neelgai are commonly seen grazing on the open sites on roadsides and banks of river and reservoir while jackals can be seen in search of food anywhere in the park. Apparently, packs of wild dogs can also be seen occasionally and Herds of Gaur can be spotted near streams and bamboo patches. You look forward to seeing them all, but it is the world famous Bengal tiger that really peaks your interest.

Chandeliers on Abbey | MARGARET RIVER, WESTERN AUSTRALIA | AUSTRALIA

The irony that privacy and seclusion are what you have come to covet most dearly is not lost on you. You are well aware of what your time is worth and quite conscious of how valuable those precious few days you get with the love of your life really are. So when an associate turned you onto to a semi-secret resort tucked between the internationally renowned wineries of Amberley and Abbey Vale, you knew this would be the location of your next sojourn. But you were not swayed by the description of the massive soaker tub or by the idea of a private plunge pool. It wasn't even the promise of a gold plate chef at your disposal every night. No. It was the description of the quaint country lane leading up to the bungalow that captured your imagination. And the assurance of the absolute privacy and seclusion you would experience within the folds of the surrounding National Forest.

Hinanoza | KUSHIRO | JAPAN

Hot spring water bubbles around you in the outdoor spa. The ice and snow covered surface of Lake Akan stretches before you, flanked by the thick native forest of the mountains. Beneath the frozen surface, 'marimo' - a unique algae that grows to the size of soccer balls - hibernates, waiting for the thaw of spring. For your refreshment, a tray of steaming herbal tea silently appears at your elbow, delivered by one of the attentive and unobtrusive staff at this traditional Japanese ryokan. As you soak in the rejuvenating mineral water, you feel the peace and the tranquillity that is 'Hinanoza', seep into your pores. Tomorrow, you'll try the heated rock baths. Relaxed, you don your 'yukata', the casual kimono you received upon arrival, and stroll back to your room. You have a date this evening at the Za bar, just you and some great jazz music.

Kuramure | OTARU | JAPAN

You and two girlfriends have returned from a weekend at Kuramure. Unlike the more traditional ryokans of the area, Kuramure was more akin to a boutique design hotel. And what design! Low, grey clad buildings, reminiscent of modern, trendy warehouse space, with a clean, simple interior of natural colours and woods. Outside the hotel, deep snow was on the ground and continuing to fall, adding a sense of muffled serenity. The tearoom was lovely and one of the girls suggested booking it for an informal tea ceremony. Too late this time, but maybe next. This trip you had already planned to take in the outdoor bath with its spectacular view over a stream (particularly striking in the snow), and to enjoy it kaiseki style which included a sample (or two) of saki. And, to top it off, you retired to the "library" area to play your hand as DJ for the night.

Punters Corner The Retreat | COONAWARRA, SOUTH AUSTRALIA | AUSTRALIA

Beyond the floor to ceiling windows in your bedroom, kookaburras laugh in the gumtrees. The rising sun dissolves the last of the frost. When you arrived the night before, the vineyard appeared ghostly silent in the moonlight. This morning, the supple green vines, laden with plump purple fruit, stretch in neat rows over the rolling hills. The timber floorboards feel smooth beneath your feet as you pad through the spacious interior of The Retreat at Punters Corner. You can't help pausing to admire the glorious views in all directions through the wall-to-wall glass. You reach the courtyard. There laid out on the wooden table is a sumptuous full breakfast, a mouth-watering welcome to Coonawarra and the wine country. You take a deep breath of the sweet country air and pull out a chair. There is time to relax and savour the beauty of this unspoilt morning. After all, the Cellar Door at Punters Corner doesn't open until ten.

KIWICOLLECTION.COM

Azur | QUEENSTOWN, SOUTH ISLAND | NEW ZEALAND

Standing on the balcony you watch as night falls over the majestic landscape. The mountains, looming shadows, and the sparkling carpet of stars stretch from horizon to horizon. The toasty warmth of the gas fire reaches out to you from the lounge. Sipping your wine you reflect on your adrenaline charged day. This morning, you held tight as the jet boat sped across the lake, waves frothing in its wake. This afternoon, you fulfilled a 20 year ambition and jumped off a cliff, plummeting hundreds of meters, your only lifeline a bungee cord. You never will forget the feel of the wind rushing past your face, or the clarity of your view of the world at that exact moment the cord snapped like an elastic band, jerking you towards the sky. For tomorrow's activities the staff at Azur have organised another adventure filled day, beginning with a helicopter ride to the surrounding peaks. Tonight, you slumber and dream.

Whare Kea Lodge | WANAKA, SOUTH ISLAND | NEW ZEALAND

Perched on the mountaintop, you feel as though you are floating above Lake Wanaka, yet surrounded by the snowy peaks of Mount Aspiring and Mount Cook. Turning away from the wall-to-wall glass and moonlit view, you smile, as three generations of your family lounge around the crackling fireplace at Whare Kea Lodge, swapping stories as they laugh and reminisce. The scent of smouldering pine logs and the passing around of steaming mugs of hot chocolate with marshmallows add to the warm family atmosphere. Grandpa is insisting that it was the largest catch, in history, that got away from him today on the river. As you watch, Grandma squeezes his shoulder and whispers softly, and Grandpa concedes. Then it's Joey's turn to wave enthusiastically as he describes how his cousins managed to capsize the canoe, plunging them all into the lake. This is your family; sharing these special moments with them is what life is all about.

Amanbagh | ALWAR, AJABGARH | INDIA

Let's face it. You want to get away from people: employees, colleagues, family - all of them. Set in isolation amidst the arid Aravalli Hills, near Alwar in northern India, the Amanbagh promises the privacy and sanctity you seek. After all the business conferences of the past year - the networking and mingling and trying to stay awake during the same old presentations, for a change, you just want to be left alone. You don't want to worry about what you are wearing or with whom you are meeting. And you do not want to see even one more business card. Needless to say, small talk, this week, is completely out of the question. You want finally to be able to read the newspaper cover to cover, at your own pace. Who knows, you may even put your feet up.

KIWICOLLECTION.COM

Bamurru Plains | KAKADU NATIONAL PARK, NORTHERN TERRITORY | AUSTRALIA
Wow. This is about as far from the typical perception of Australian wilderness as you can imagine. Water, water, everywhere! These floodplains of the Mary River are enormous and house an astounding variety of birds and land creatures. And what a way to experience it. The airboat tour was awesome – tomorrow's river cruise to view the crocs will be hard pressed to be more exciting. They say they're all about 'wild bush luxury', and they'll get no arguments from you – simple, understated luxury – just the way you like it. With the day's activities behind you, it's now naptime - just a short one, of course. You won't want to miss sunset and the gradual silencing of the creatures as they rest up to put on their spectacular show again tomorrow, for more of Bamurru's guests.

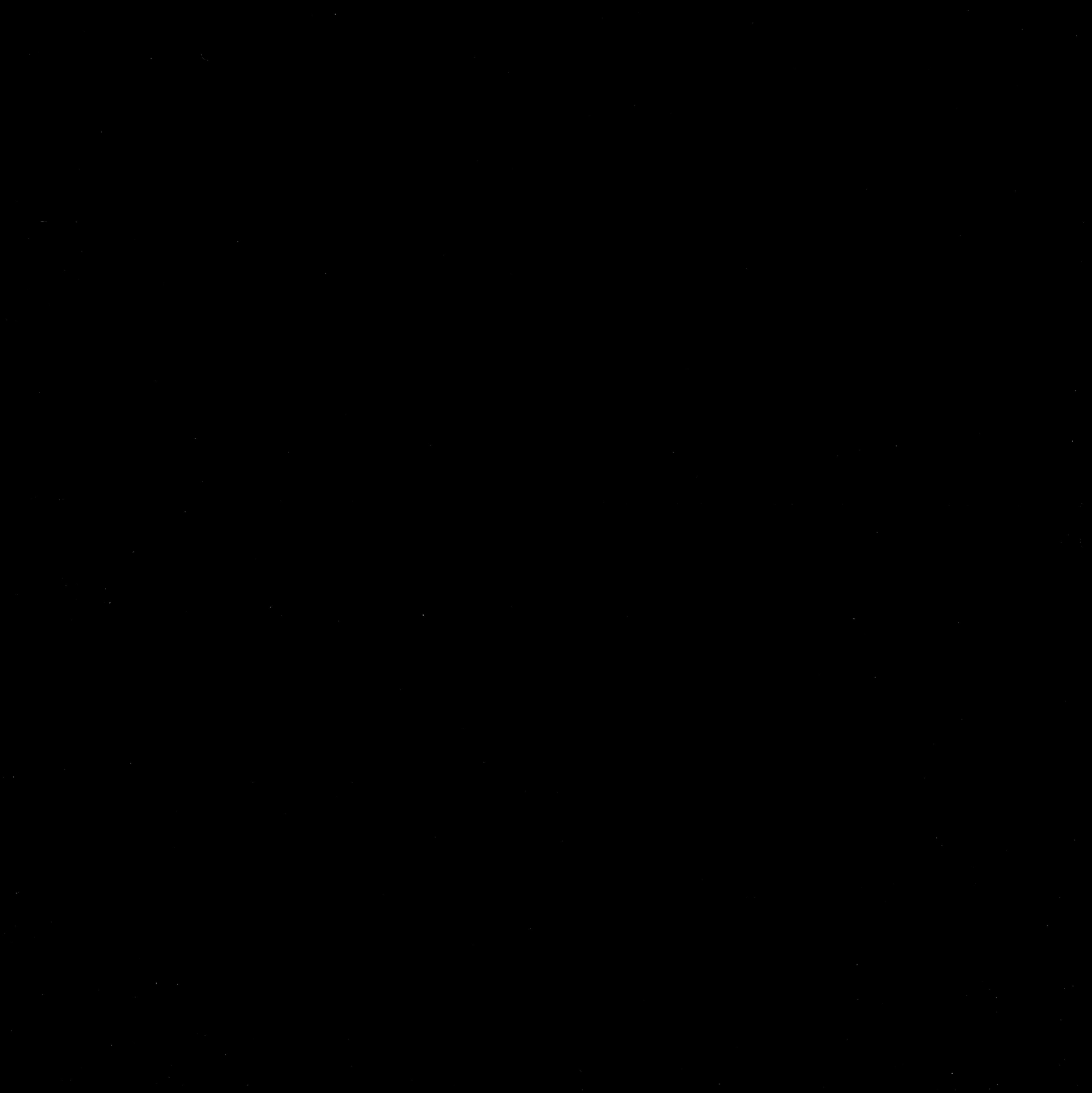

CITY

InterContinental Hong Kong | HONG KONG, S.A.R. | CHINA

Not usually one to be swayed by the ratings and rankings you read in magazines, you prefer to draw conclusions about quality, performance, and luxury from personal experience. And now, taking in the view of Hong Kong's Victoria Harbour with a perfectly poured martini in hand, you have no choice but to agree with the cadre of magazine editors who have named this one of the best hotels in the world. Not only is it consistently ranked among the best, it's one of your favourites and it is home to what you think must be one of the sexiest and hippest presidential suites in existence: 7000 square feet of unapologetic opulence, luxury, and sophistication. And, while you may not be staying here for long, if the deal you have been working on for the last six months is finalised in the morning, you might very well be staying here a bit longer.

The Oberoi Grand, Kolkata | KOLKATA, WEST BENGAL | INDIA

You were surprised and honoured by the invitation to attend the Consular General's daughter's wedding. When you mentioned that you were staying at The Oberoi Grand, he insisted that you share in the event. After all, the wedding celebrations were being held at your hotel. Leaving the consulate, all thoughts of diplomatic discussion dissipate as you contemplate how you will find a suitable outfit for the wedding, a gift for the bride and groom, and look your best at such short notice. Entering the foyer, the hotel staff greets you and you find yourself telling them of your challenge. They give you a reassuring smile and usher you to The Oberoi Grand's exclusive boutiques. You leave perfectly outfitted for the grand occasion, with a superb gift for the wedding party in-hand. Finally, an appointment at the luxurious Oberoi Spa and Fitness Centre by Banyan Tree promises to have you relaxed and looking your best before the event.

Eight Nicholson Subiaco | PERTH-SUBIACO, WESTERN AUSTRALIA | AUSTRALIA

You're fine with being the convention's keynote speaker, especially in Perth, one of your favourite cities, but at the end of the day you want escape: to park your Pradas somewhere that's not host to the latest wanna-be billionaire looking to profit from your financial prowess. With only four rooms, the Eight Nicholson suits you fine, and it's just down the street from trendy Subiaco. It's sort of like that 1920s house in Beverly Hills you can't bear to part with, combined with your favourite King's Road nightclub, the one that never lets in riff-raff. And when called on, Eight Nicholson will promptly cater a breakfast meeting, letting you concentrate on business at hand over a warm croissant. While out shopping for shoes in Subiaco, you're stopped by someone who recognises your picture from the Financial Times. No worries. You smile and hold out a loafer. "Fetch me these in a size 44, please."

Four Seasons Hotel Bangkok | BANGKOK | THAILAND

You arrived at the Four Seasons Hotel Bangkok well after midnight. It had been a long day of travelling and your exhaustion was evident. Despite the late hour of your arrival, you were greeted at the check-in desk as cheerfully as if it were ten in the morning. In spite of your exhaustion and the great comfort the serene room provided, you were restless from the long flight and found yourself lying wide awake at 4:30AM. Happily, hotel room service is available at any hour and your order for tea arrived within minutes, beautifully presented in fine china with white linens. As grueling as the long travel to Bangkok can sometimes be, you are always happy to return; you know how pleasant and accommodating the staff at the Four Seasons will be at any hour of the day.

BLUE Sydney | SYDNEY, NEW SOUTH WALES | AUSTRALIA

On a recent business trip to the city, you stayed for five nights at the BLUE Sydney. The unique architecture (the hotel itself is a beautifully restored old wharf building mixed with sleek and modern interior design and cleverly hidden lighting) offered an industrial, yet comforting, setting. Your room too was modern, with clean lines and a huge writing desk (which was perfect for working). Your secretary had booked you a loft style room with the living area downstairs and the bedroom and bath upstairs. Just like home. Last night you were pleased to check out the bar (your secretary said it was voted one of the top bars in Sydney) and tonight you will stroll the neighbourhood and have a look at some of the many restaurants that the area has to offer.

The Ritz-Carlton Beijing, Financial Street | BEIJING, MUNICIPALITY OF BEIJING | CHINA

After a week of grueling 10-hour days, going from merger meeting to lawyer's office and back again, it is nice to unwind and relax at The Ritz-Carlton Beijing, Financial Street. Conveniently located in the heart of the financial district, within its walls, it is removed enough to provide a much needed respite from business. A drink or two before dinner in the lounge on the club level is a convenient stop on the way to your room. And, this evening, more business meetings, certainly. That is, after all, why you are here. But the merger negotiations are complete and tonight will be according to your own schedule, for a change. With everything having gone so well, a celebration of sorts is in order. Accordingly, you have invited your lawyers to meet you in the hotel restaurant, Qi, for your favourite celebratory meal in Beijing – Peking Duck.

The Fullerton Hotel Singapore | SINGAPORE | SINGAPORE

Tea time in the cathedral-like atrium of The Fullerton. Shafts of afternoon sunshine pierce the glazed roof and dapple the marble floor in pools of light; a string quartet is playing Mozart, with an exquisite touch; and all around, rising and falling, the reassuring hum of conversation, the gentle chorus of contented living. Over cake and biscuits, you're reading about this grand and endlessly fascinating hotel, tracing its descent from the 1920s. If ever there was a building for all seasons, a hotel for all styles, tastes, and occasions, this is it. As you read, the hotel yields its secrets. The 'Fullerton Lighthouse', you discover, is not just a quaint name for the rooftop restaurant; in a former life it was indeed a beacon, guiding ships into Singapore. You imagine the view of the city by night, boats moving like fireflies across the black canvas of the water, the harbour aflame with colour. Tonight, when you dine, you'll be a lighthouse keeper.

CITY 133

The Ritz-Carlton, Jakarta | JAKARTA, JAVA | INDONESIA

Is there anything more decadent than breakfast in bed? At home you would never think of such a thing, let alone allow it in any of your rooms. Dirty dishes in the bedroom and crumbs in the bed – what would the kids think? Still, a vacation would not be a vacation, in the true sense of the word, without at least one morning meal served and eaten in the comfort of your sleeping quarters. Fortunately, your husband knows about this little desire of yours and has made the necessary arrangements so that, today, you have awoken in The Ritz-Carlton, Jakarta to a breakfast tray of exotic fresh fruits, steaming hot coffee, and an assortment of decadent breakfast pastries. Let the vacation begin!

Hotel Lindrum | MELBOURNE, VICTORIA | AUSTRALIA

Delirious with joy you return to the Hotel Lindrum humming a show tune. The concierge was correct in his recommendations for the evening's entertainment, and helpful, at the last minute, in acquiring two tickets to the sold out musical. Your partner is still smiling, enjoyment of the evening obvious. Pausing in the lobby you share an embrace and a whispered conversation. You agree to continue this magical night in the Lindrum Bar. You lounge on supple leather armchairs by the open fireplace; logs crackle and glow as soft music floats on the air. You savour your cognac, hands entwined as you reminisce over your favourite moments in the show. Soon, the two of you will retire to the warm wood furnishings and muted lighting of your suite, a private members' club just for two.

Metropolitan Bangkok | BANGKOK | THAILAND

The truth is, you know good art when you see it. Over the years, this has made you a savvy collector. Art imbues every part of your life: the clothes you wear, the towels in your bathroom. Granted, your partners find this a bit irritating (though they found it charming when they met you) and yes, it makes you a tad particular when it comes to choosing a hotel. When shopping for antiquities in Bangkok, the Metropolitan is your home away from home. The Kathryn King-designed penthouse suite is exquisite in every detail, from the Isometrix lighting to the oxidised brass panelling. Staff are dressed in Yohji Yamamoto, and the Natee Utarit paintings give depth to the clean spaces. You've come to Bangkok looking for art; but instead, you find you have become it.

JW Marriott Kuala Lumpur | KUALA LUMPUR | MALAYSIA

From the moment the chauffeur opened your door and you alighted from the limousine, you could feel the energy of the Golden Triangle. Your hotel is in the heart of this pulsing business district. Cultural and historical sights, and prime shopping venues are all within walking distance. The leisure concierge greets you by name as you pause to pick up tomorrow's itinerary for that privately guided tour of the vibrant city of Kuala Lumpur. Your table for two at the Satay Club has been confirmed for tonight, your mouth watering in anticipation of another delicious dinner. There is just enough time, before your reservation, to enjoy a pre-dinner cocktail in the hotel's JW Lounge on the 24th floor, where you both can watch the city skyline come to sparkling life as the sun sets over this magnificent city.

Hotel Seiyo Ginza | TOKYO | JAPAN

Your new assistant booked you into the Hotel Seiyo Ginza for the four nights you would be staying in Tokyo while attending a series of business meetings. As it was your first time in Tokyo, you were hopeful that the hotel (and the city itself) would live up to everything you've heard. Fortunately, (or unfortunately depending on how you look at it) your assistant knows you well enough to know your weakness for fashion shopping. Why else would she have placed you right in the heart of the Ginza district, Tokyo's most famous upmarket shopping area? With some of your favourites, like Barney's New York and Matsuya, within walking distance, it's a good thing your hotel room has walk-in closets – you will likely be needing the extra space for all your purchases.

Langham Hotel | MELBOURNE, VICTORIA | AUSTRALIA

You're a patron of pleasure, a connoisseur of comfort. That's why you're imagining yourself as a hotel inspector. The Langham, you decide, will submit to your forensic eye and your unyielding pursuit of quality. And when your survey is complete, you'll award the hotel a mark for excellence. You admire the huge Waterford crystal chandelier in the foyer, shimmering in the light. A good first impression. You open the door to your room and sigh at the immaculate presentation and the magnificent view across the Yarra River. Next, having tested the bed and smiled contentedly, you head for the spa health suite. Will it live up to its own lavish publicity? After ticking all the superlatives in the brochure, you confirm that mind, body, and soul are handsomely served. Two days later, relaxed and rehabilitated, you check out. As your cab leaves, a puzzled maid finds the sheet of paper on the bedside table. All it says is '10'. Nothing more, nothing less.

The Strand | YANGON | MYANMAR

From the moment you arrived at The Strand, and the soft sounds of Burmese music filled the lobby, you felt as though you had stepped back in time to the 1920s. Enveloped in the chivalrous charm of the colonial style of your surroundings and effortless efficiency of the attentive staff you don't hesitate to indulge your desires. Teakwood floors gleam beneath your feet, a reminder of the mysterious history of Yangon - a curious mix of British Colonialism and Buddhism and the competing British and Burmese factions who fought to control the lucrative trade in teak. Entering the Strand Bar you find yourself in a bygone era of jazz and seductive cocktails. The two-piece band comes to a swinging finish as you order a martini at the dimly lit bar. Raising your glass you nod to the saxophonist. "Play it again, Sam."

Alila Jakarta | JAKARTA, JAVA | INDONESIA

Your boss is panicking, the success of the bid is hanging in the balance. You take a deep breath and leave the meeting room to return to your executive suite. From the moment you arrived with your colleagues and were greeted by the smiling friendly team at Alila Jakarta, you felt everything would be safely taken care of. Here, nothing is impossible and the staff work enthusiastically, with effortless grace, towards providing for all your needs, both business and personal. Be confident, select what you require from your suite, don't be distracted, just yet, by the historical and cultural landmarks beyond the floor to ceiling windows. Return to the elevators and head to the hotel's business centre, where the wealth of business services available will be invaluable in assisting you to rescue your team's bid for that highly profitable contract. This business trip is turning out to be, surprisingly, refreshing and successful at the same time.

Hotel Mulia Senayan | JAKARTA, JAVA | INDONESIA

The professional demands of your job require constant travel and, as a result, you have developed a sophisticated international palette. Whether at breakfast, lunch, or dinner you always make the effort to indulge in the regional cuisine of your international hosts. However, there are times when you have an urge for something simple; something that reminds you of home: a perfect peach, a plump plum, a handful of succulent cherries. And after two weeks on the road, this morning is one of those moments. As casually you peruse one of the most impressive breakfast buffets you have ever seen, you are tempted by waffles, muesli, omelets, croissants, and even Nasi Goreng. But none of those will do the trick. Then at the end of the table you eye exactly what you are hunting: a basket of perfectly shaped peaches with a gorgeous golden hue. Sometimes, you think to yourself with a smile, the simplest things really do satisfy most.

The Taj Mahal Palace & Tower | MUMBAI, MAHARASHTRA | INDIA

Your bare toes sink into the hand-woven silk carpet as you step beneath the graceful curve of an alabaster archway in your suite. The intimate alcove overlooks the choppy water of the Arabian Sea. Deftly, the butler pulls out your chair as you sit at the table laid out with a gleaming pewter tea service and plates of petite Indian delicacies. At your nod, white gloved hands gently pour steaming golden liquid into a porcelain teacup. Discretely, the butler dissolves into the background leaving you to contemplate the cultural abundance of Mumbai. Here, in The Taj Mahal Palace & Tower, you are indulged in the sumptuous splendour of a bygone era; your every wish diligently fulfilled by the attentive staff. Your royal fantasy complete, you sip your tea. The butler has already excused himself, leaving for the opulent bathroom to draw your bath.

Hyatt Regency Kyoto | KYOTO | JAPAN

With only a few days to spend in Kyoto you considered it mandatory to stay in the city's cultural heart. The Hyatt Regency Kyoto was the obvious choice. The hotel's blend of traditional Japanese style with acclaimed modern design immediately was striking. Yesterday you toured Kyoto's most famous temples: Sanjusangendo, Chisakuin, and Yogenin. However, today has you seeking another kind of religious experience. A treatment in the Hyatt Regency's RIRAKU Spa followed by an exquisite Japanese meal at Touzan, one of the hotel's three exemplary restaurants, sounds like a great way to start your day - before you head to the famed Kyoto National Museum. Remembering that at the end of your day you will be able to relax in your suite's deep Japanese bath, you make the ambitious plan to schedule a walk through the Gion District early tomorrow, before you leave, with the hope you may catch a rare glimpse of one of Kyoto's beautiful Geisha on her way to work.

Amangalla | GALLE | SRI LANKA

If you are looking for a world-class spa experience and, let's face it, who isn't these days, then Amangalla in Sri Lanka is as good a place as any from which to begin your search. Located in the historic and traditional town of Galle, the Baths at Amangalla offer the luxuriance of a distant age through using world-famous Sri Lankan Ayurvedic healing traditions to revitalise the body and sooth the spirit. Bath houses go back to ancient times in Sri Lanka; but with his and her full day treatments that include the use of hydrotherapy pools, steam and sauna rooms, cold plunge pools, and a relaxation room - followed by a champagne and lobster lunch for two served in the garden by Amangalla's pool - the concept of ancient bath houses has taken on a whole new, and very welcome, meaning.

The Dharmawangsa | JAKARTA, JAVA | INDONESIA

You trail your fingers through the iridescent water and nibble on a light fluffy pastry as you recline on a comfortable sun lounger beside the pool at The Dharmawangsa. Fresh from the Cake Shop in the lobby, the sugary concoction dissolves on your tongue. Trees, their boughs bent, reach across the pool; their leafy arms providing intervals of shade and a teasing rustle in the breeze. Closing your eyes you drift off, completely at home, as if you are an honoured family guest in a private residence. Your snooze is gently interrupted by the butler. It is time to adjourn to your suite in preparation for the afternoon's board meeting in the hotel's Singosari meeting room. How easy it was to forget work amongst the rich Indonesian furnishings and quiet solitude of your surroundings. Refreshed from your poolside sojourn, your fingers dip one last time beneath the water before you turn towards your suite.

Raffles Hotel Singapore | SINGAPORE | SINGAPORE

The latest fashion trend? Seen it. Minimalist architecture? Not interested. What truly matters is style, timeless style, the kind that puts on a Chanel suit, goes to the bullfight, and pours a short neat scotch at the end of the day. This is why at the end of your business travels, you make a much-needed stop at the Raffles Hotel Singapore. Here you're back in a gentler time, one inspired by colonial bungalows of the early 20th century, with Oriental carpets and 5 metre high ceilings. Sitting on the verandah, you watch magenta bougainvillea blossoms drift by on a passing breeze, half-expecting someone to ride up on a bicycle and shout out a cheery greeting. This place has been around for over a hundred years, and it's not going anywhere soon. It's of a style that never goes out of style.

KIWICOLLECTION.COM

Mollies | AUCKLAND, NORTH ISLAND | NEW ZEALAND

In the lavish dining room at Mollies, the symphony orchestra builds to a volatile crescendo and then, silence. Someone gasps, a collective shiver races through the guests seated around the long dining table. The lights, dramatically low to cast mysterious shadows around the room, set the scene. The soulful strains of a single violin float into the room. Friendly chatter resumes as glasses of ruby red or gold liquid are sipped. Outside, the evening breeze teases the trees in the courtyard into a leafy dance as the expectant atmosphere, inside, grows. A flicker of the lights, then darkness. Your friend to your right giggles nervously. A flare of light: miniature candles, burning brightly on a bed of chocolate frosting, are placed before you. Around you your friends begin to sing, off-key mostly. Taking a deep breath you make a wish. The lights flicker to life. You wink at the perpetrator of tonight's theatrics. The Butler did it.

The Prince | MELBOURNE, VICTORIA | AUSTRALIA

The partially opened blinds send bands of light across the ceiling, down the wall, your partner, only minimally clothed, surrendered to an afternoon nap after a day exploring the St. Kilda District. It's tempting to wake this stunning creature, but instead you retire to the other room and have a soak in the Philippe Starck tub. Everything about The Prince is minimalist, free of clutter, hot and cool at the same time. Just the way you like it. "Darling?" you here from the doorway. "I'm hungry. Let's go out." Fully clothed of course, it will have to be. After dinner and a cocktail at The Prince's underground vodka bar, you're both half-undressed by the time you get back to your room. Your jacket lands on the floor in a pile. Another time you would hang it up. But not tonight. Tonight it's okay if things get a little messy.

KIWICOLLECTION.COM

Establishment Hotel | SYDNEY, NEW SOUTH WALES | AUSTRALIA

You've always been of two minds about everything, which is why you chose the Establishment Hotel for your trip to Sydney. You're here for two reasons: rest and revelry. Just like you, the hotel is a two-sided coin - old and modern, trendy and sophisticated. Even the rooms come in one of two colour palettes: bold or tranquil. It is just as you heard, quiet on weekdays so you can relax and take in the sights of the Opera House and harbour, and active on weekends, when local "scenesters" converge on the premises. You decide to join them, dining at the famous restaurant, Est., one night and nibbling on the award-winning sushi at Sushi e, the next. A drink at the outdoor garden bar and a spin at the neighbouring nightclub, and you're ready to turn in. A plate of warm cookies on your bed greets your arrival. Yes, you marvel, here you can have your cake and eat it too.

W Seoul Walkerhill | SEOUL | SOUTH KOREA

Dear G: Arriving at the W Seoul is like entering a fantastical cloud floating on the side of Mount Acha overlooking the Han River. We feel as though we have stepped into a six-course feast for the senses. The white on white rooms come alive with bold splashes of colour that invigorate and delight the eyes. Because we are situated close to the financial district, T successfully has completed the business end of our trip. Now we both can relax and enjoy this unique destination set in the parklands of Seoul. Even Jock, our Scottish terrier, is feeling indulged and pampered by the exclusive treatment at the W. Upon arrival, he was presented with his very own pet bed and doggy toy. The maids here spoil him terribly with tasty turndown treats in the evenings. Tomorrow we plan to practice our swings at the golf range. Each night we return to our room replete from our experiences at the W.

JIA Boutique Hotel | HONG KONG, S.A.R. | CHINA

You simply adore Hong Kong – the vibrant energy, the lights, the shopping, the dining, and the endless walking. And now that you have stayed at the JIA Boutique Hotel, you love this fantastic city just a little bit more. Your suite, with its kitchenette and more than adequate storage space, was really more of a bijou apartment, if truth be told, and was an oasis in the middle of the city. The hotel itself was just the right blend of funky, friendly, and charming with simple, but stylish, decor and very thoughtful attention to detail. From the 'Luxe Guide to Hong Kong' that you found in your room, in one sitting you were able to plan out the next five days: where to eat, where to walk, and of course, where to get your custom shirts and suits tailored.

The Ritz-Carlton, Seoul | SEOUL | SOUTH KOREA

In a city of business hotels, The Ritz-Carlton may very well be the only true luxury hotel to be found. And you should know, you've stayed here over ten times in the past two years. What you like about The Ritz-Carlton, Seoul is its consistency – the décor is stylish and consistently exudes quality. The rooms are decorated in a classical style that you find very pleasing. The furniture is of fine quality and is solid and interesting, the pictures on the walls are limited edition signed copies of original paintings, the lamps are made from beautiful pottery, a CD player with classical and jazz CDs is provided, the quality of bed linens and curtains is top notch. In fact, the overall impression within the hotel is of comfort, quality, and style.

The Ritz-Carlton, Kuala Lumpur | KUALA LUMPUR | MALAYSIA

As you float in the balmy aqua pool of your tropical oasis, palm trees vie with white fluffy clouds for space in the cobalt blue sky overhead. You wiggle your toes in the silky water fully recovered from yesterday's 'shop till you drop marathon' that began at Bintang Walk and culminated at the Central Market, satisfied with the beautiful batik pieces and Malaysian handicrafts for which you expertly haggled. Today you chose to relax, allowing the golden sun to melt your bones and the serenity of your surroundings to seep into your soul. Your every whim is indulged by attentive staff at the poolside bar of The Ritz-Carlton, Kuala Lumpur. For lunch, definitely the green papaya and chilli prawn salad followed by a refreshing mango, lychee, and mint fruit dessert; but first, a very short espresso to kick-off this glorious day.

CITY 151

Park Hyatt Melbourne | MELBOURNE, VICTORIA | AUSTRALIA

Sweat dripping from your brow, muscles burning, you leave Fitzroy Gardens and jog the remaining distance to the Park Hyatt. Dusk slips into evening and the city springs into dazzling light around you. Pausing at the concierge's desk, as you make your way to your suite, you nod in gratitude as the attendant hands you a towel and a bottle of water. Invigorated, muscles aching in a good way, you take a long hot soak in the Italian marble bath, before relaxing on your balcony overlooking the beautiful old St Patrick's Cathedral. The phone rings; you pick up the extension. Shrugging on your dinner jacket your leave to meet your guests below at Radii's Restaurant and Bar. As you approach the restaurant, your mouth starts to water. The appetizing aromas rising from the open kitchen dictate a more rapid pace.

KIWICOLLECTION.COM

The Peninsula Hong Kong | HONG KONG, S.A.R. | CHINA

Like a giant bird of prey, the helicopter swoops through the dramatic high-rises of Hong Kong before landing deftly on the rooftop helipad at The Peninsula. Attendants assist you from your seat. You are lead directly to your suite where you can work on your business notes and relax, in luxurious grandeur, amidst the soft elegant furnishings and unique oriental pieces. Soon it will be time to dress for this evening's festivities. For now, you are content to watch as the butler directs the staff in arranging the covered terrace for tonight's dinner party. The long gleaming oak table is set with sparkling crystal and silverware. Stylish tapered candles burn brightly between vases of lilies and jonquils. To the side, a cello player prepares her instrument with a final tune of the strings. It will be a night of celebration and elegant dining, a fitting reward for your team's hard work and loyalty.

Shangri-La Hotel, Singapore | SINGAPORE | SINGAPORE

When you decided to break your journey to Sydney with a night at the Shangri-La Hotel, Singapore, little did you know it would be more heart stopping than pit stop. From the moment you enter the building, the grandeur and sophistication of your Singapore staging post is arresting. The cavernous lobby and open-air atrium, complete with marble pillars, cascading waterfall and exotic plants, leaves you standing in wonder. Then, as you gaze through windows the size of polar ice sheets, you see for the first time the stunning scale of the surrounding garden. Yes, this hotel has its own private estate, its own 15-acre botanical park. Your eye is drawn to the eccentrically-shaped swimming pool fringed with palm trees, a striking focus amid the lush vegetation and beautiful landscaping. Sadly, you're only passing through enroute to Australia; this is not a destination, just a magnificent diversion. But then again, there's always the return journey…

KIWICOLLECTION.COM

CITY 155

D2hotel chiang mai | CHIANG MAI | THAILAND

Located in Chiang Mai's famous night market, a fifteen minute walk from the Old Town and about five to ten minutes from the Ping River, D2hotel is a perfect base point from which to explore Thailand's vibrant Chiang Mai. This true walking city, with an abundance of fantastic restaurants and unique shops, can keep even the most experienced traveller fascinated for days on end. After a day of seemingly endless exploring through tiny side streets and crowded main avenues, (and when your feet just couldn't take it anymore, a most interesting, and just a little unnerving, tuk-tuk ride through the traffic laden core), you head back to the hotel with your new found purchases. Your goal: to top it all off with a cool clear martini at the outdoor bar and to hit the night market and start the shopping and walking all over again.

Seikoro Inn | TOKYO | JAPAN

The best part of the Seikoro Inn, and the reason you just keep coming back time after time, is its ability to maintain a fresh, yet traditional, existence in the midst of the ever changing and constantly expanding city of Kyoto. The building itself dates back over a century. With its spectacular old-world front gate leading into a small Japanese courtyard, it is possibly one of the most charming entryways you have seen in Japan thus far. The hotel offers a glimpse of an antique Japan, replete with the country's fascinating culture and history, but is so conveniently located in the heart of the city that you don't have to miss out on the 21st century aspects of Kyoto that are just as fascinating in their own right.

The Scarlet Hotel | SINGAPORE | SINGAPORE

Your presentation was a rousing success. The client signed off your campaign, budgets, everything, on the spot. Striding out of the boardroom you refer to the leather wallet your assistant handed you this morning. "The Scarlet Hotel", you say, as you lean into the open window of the taxi. Instead of opening the door for you, the driver simply looks impressed and points to a magnificently stylish building only doors from the advertising agency. Perfect. As you enter the stylish foyer, you're then drawn to the plush trappings of The Scarlet Hotel's bar and find yourself seated at the cool black marble bar amongst Singapore's trendiest. Sipping on a glass of champagne and enjoying a mouth watering selection of canapés, you enjoy a moment to celebrate your success. Soon your mind turns to rewarding yourself at the eclectic mix of shops, wine bars, and art galleries that beckon outside. Ahhh, success is sweet.

The Westin Melbourne | MELBOURNE, VICTORIA | AUSTRALIA

A "girls weekend" in Melbourne – what a fabulous idea! Although not exactly an original one since the five of you have been getting together for these annual girl's weekends for the past four years. And as has become the custom since the onset of these getaways, you all will be staying at The Westin Melbourne. Every one of you loves the hotel as much as you love Melbourne itself. Conveniently located right in the heart of the city's famous theatre district, with close access to boutique shopping centres, art galleries (in case someone is feeling cultural), fantastic restaurants and bars, and, of course, Federation Square, The Westin Melbourne provides the ideal location from which the five of you can shop, wine, and dine your way through a decadent (but very much deserved) ladies-only weekend.

Adelphi Hotel | MELBOURNE, VICTORIA | AUSTRALIA

From the moment you arrived at the converted warehouse that is your destination you were stunned and inspired by its clean, minimalist, and fresh design. Staying here is a very special experience: the feeling of space and simplicity is enriched by the generous attention to comfort and the efficient discreet staff. You can appreciate why the Adelphi Hotel, has received international acclaim for its architectural design and vision. Of course you didn't forget to pack your swimsuit and goggles. Soon you'll be ready for a trip to the rooftop pool deck and some extra-special fun, a dive into the crystal clear water and a wave to the people on Flinders Lane below; after all, you have an unimpeded view through the transparent Perspex bottom of the pool. How cheeky!

The Chedi, Chiang Mai | CHIANG MAI | THAILAND

Forget all your expectations. Arriving at The Chedi, you step into your own private oasis amidst the colourful noisy bustle of the city of Chiang Mai. The clock winds back to a forgotten era as you sit within the hotel's dining room. You partake of the traditional high tea service, housed in the historic second building, a stark contrast to the modernity and amenities of the main building. In the evening, you follow the flickering path of floating candles, set among the lily pads, to the private courtyard entrance of your spacious room. Inside, you pull on the plush bathrobe before slipping out to the balcony to admire the night sky from the comfort of the daybed. You have left the world behind and discovered your own wonderland in this mix of the old and the new.

The Sukhothai | BANGKOK | THAILAND

Mobile phone switched off. This is it, your chance to escape. Last night's sumptuous banquet in the hotel's ballroom is a happy memory as you retreat through the gardens, past the lotus ponds, of The Sukhothai. Follow the soothing sound of tinkling water to your individual suite of tranquillity, a harmonious blend of teak and soft fabrics. Drop the briefcase and those shopping bags. Feel yourself relaxing? You're ready to be pampered and spoilt from head to toe at The Sukhothai Spa. How do you choose just a few of the indulgent treatments from the Beauty Menu? There's the 'King's Bath', the 'Mud Pool' or, maybe, a 'Guava and Mango Body Scrub'. Hmmm. But you don't have to decide. You have time to experience them all. And don't forget cocktails in the Salon followed by another gourmet meal of Thai delicacies. This is bliss.

Four Seasons Hotel Tokyo at Marunouchi | TOKYO | JAPAN

Your mind knows what it's supposed to hear. In this case it should be a train whizzing by – the clacking of steel on steel, the Doppler effect of approach and retreat, the swoosh of a curtain of air. Instead, what you hear is absolutely nothing. Four Seasons Hotel Tokyo at Marunouchi overlooks the train tracks - lying on your bed, watching the trains approach in a gently sweeping arc, it's a surreal sensation, almost as if you were sitting in the first few rows of a theater watching the spectacle unfold right outside your window. One of the smallest property in their portfolio, Four Seasons has truly managed to make this city hotel feel like an urban ryokan. The show's not over, but as you start to fade into a pleasant dream world, memories of the rhythmic motion of train trips long past lull you to sleep.

Rambagh Palace | JAIPUR, RAJASTHAN | INDIA

After an exhilarating, but exhausting, day of fighting your way through the teeming carnival of Jaipur street life, you have a new appreciation for why this is called India's "Pink City", and more importantly, why it is so important to have booked a room at such an exquisite hotel as the Rambagh Palace. Here at the Rambagh, the illusion of Rajasthan's "princely" heritage lives on. During the heat of the day, you are happy to wander aimlessly, amongst the crowds, through the many colourful and lively streets. You are keen to explore and discover the unique and sometimes unusual quirks of such a vibrant and busy city. However, by the time evening comes, it is nice to know you can retire in the same surroundings, and take advantage of the same comforts, that have housed generations of royals and elite.

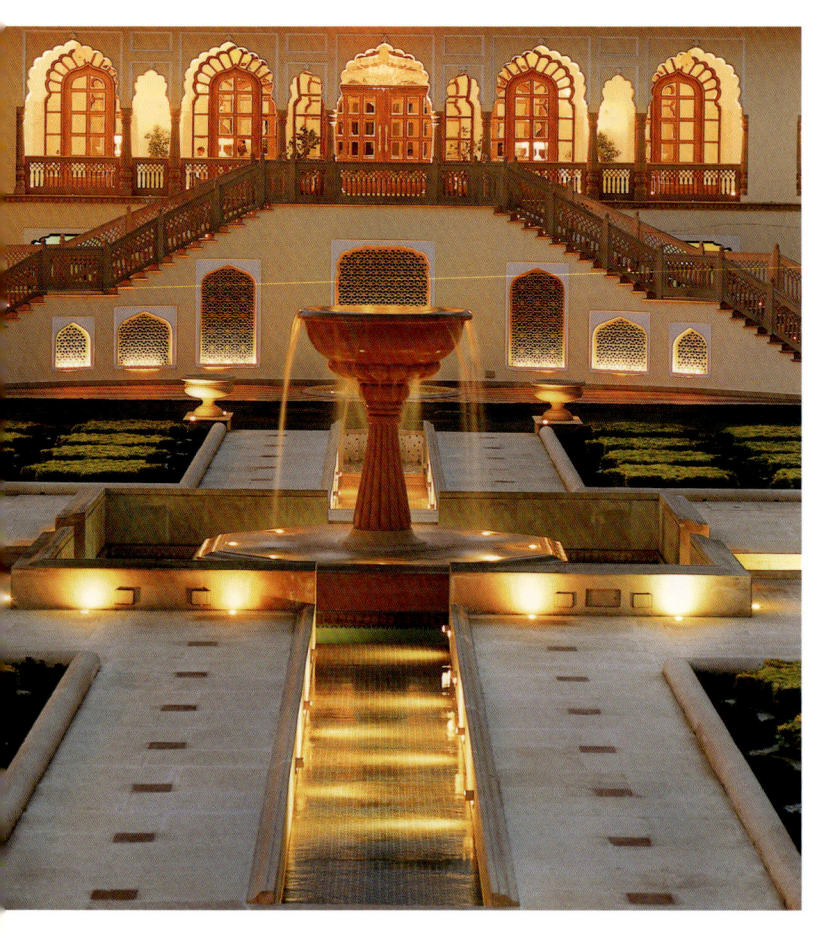

Hilton Auckland | AUCKLAND, NORTH ISLAND | NEW ZEALAND

You race to the end of the outdoor heated pool, colliding with your partner as you reach the unique viewing window that forms one side of the pool. As you both sink to the tiled floor, you wave through the transparent glass at the cruise ship gliding along Auckland Harbour. Bobbing to the surface, you recognise that twinkle in blue eyes. Twisting, you make a dash for the far end of the pool; breathless, your fingers touch smooth tiles a moment before another hand reaches past your shoulder. Laughing, victorious, you wink at your partner. There are two options for this evening's entertainment. You can explore the many funky bars and restaurants along Prince's Wharf that the concierge has recommended. Alternatively, you could order from the exceptional room service menu, and enjoy your partner's company in the comfort of your corner suite overlooking the harbour. You sigh softly as your partner takes your hand; your choice is made.

Shangri-La Hotel, The Marina, Cairns | CAIRNS, QUEENSLAND | AUSTRALIA

Like always, you've come to Cairns for business - a medical convention that promises to be as long and tedious as your flight. When you get to the hotel, you're pleasantly surprised by the view of the boats moored in the marina. Yes, this is a nice change of pace. You walk into your room on the new Horizon Floor and marvel at the accommodations. With a clean minimalist décor and a glass-walled bathroom, the blue water beyond your room provides the only splash of colour. With only a few hours before your meeting, you decide to take a stroll. Amazingly, the hotel is right next to everything - shopping, bars, restaurants on the pier. You walk around as in a daze looking at signs advertising trips to the Great Barrier Reef. As you settle on the boardwalk with a drink and watch the boats glide past, a thought begins to form. "Are you here for the convention?" a voice from behind interrupts your reverie. You take a moment and smile at the stranger. "What convention?" you ask.

The Como Melbourne | MELBOURNE, VICTORIA | AUSTRALIA

In the Musk Suite, at The Como, the tinkling sound of laughter blends intimately with the haunting tones of the grand piano. Suspended from the ceiling, a canopy of stars glitters overhead. In shadowed corners, people lounge indulgently on couches; mock orange trees affording nooks of scented privacy. Locked in your partner's embrace you gracefully glide across the dance floor. Twirling, the long pearl white satin train wraps around both of you, binding, two hearts beating as one. By the marble fireplace your elderly aunt has cornered your partner's newly single godfather. Uh oh. Poor man. Your partner caresses the back of your neck and everyone else is forgotten. Only the two of you locked in this magical moment. Around you white liveried waiters move discretely among the guests, refreshing champagne flutes and serving savoury canapés. Eyes search the room, as friends and family raise their glasses in salute to the happy couple. You've already slipped away.

The Governor's Residence | YANGON | MYANMAR

The Governor's Residence is the epitome of what you have come to expect of your vacations in Yangon (although, you can't stop thinking of the city as Rangoon, despite the name change): old style colonial charm in a blissful and serene setting. It is because of hotels such as this that you continuously return to Myanmar. Surrounded by lotus ponds, leafy gardens, and a fan-shaped swimming pool; and extravagantly catered to by knowledgeable and helpful staff, you are easily at peace here. And after day trips of exploration: excursions to Angkor Wat, the Shwedagon Pagoda (as well as countless others), and the awe-inspiring World Heritage surroundings where you discover and re-discover the cultural diversity and history of the area, peace and tranquility atop a sunbed by the pool is a welcome retreat.

The Peninsula Palace Beijing | BEIJING, MUNICIPALITY OF BEIJING | CHINA

From the moment the hotel Rolls Royce ghosted into view at the airport, you knew that Beijing would beguile you. Your plan was to blend East with West, to mix the better of two worlds, the better of two contrasting cultures, in one city and one building. That's why you chose The Peninsula Palace. Or did it choose you? You smile as you remember the words inside the fortune cookie; the message that said you would soon travel to a distant land and be treated like a king in an oriental palace, a palace with every western luxury that you could imagine or desire. Here, in the heart of Beijing, with Tiananmen Square and the Forbidden City a stroll away, that promise unfolds. Suddenly, you believe in Chinese magic. Could your luck get any better? What will tomorrow bring? Time for another fortune cookie.

Raffles Beijing Hotel | BEIJING, MUNICIPALITY OF BEIJING | CHINA

Having stayed at the famous Raffles Hotel in Singapore (and having thoroughly enjoyed it) you were eager to experience the Raffles Beijing Hotel. The lobby and the rooms of this grand hotel were just what you would expect from a five star property, with a staff that appeared to be well in tune with its guest's every need. The hotel was superbly located, with many of the city's famous landmarks just a few minutes walk away. And the concierge was extremely helpful, and knowledgeable as to the local restaurants and how best to get place to place. Upon your request, he arranged for a private car for the day to take you to the Mutian Yu area of the Great Wall and to the Ming Tombs - definitely the highlight of your fantastic Beijing vacation.

The Oriental, Bangkok | BANGKOK | THAILAND

Close your eyes and make a wish. Now open them, what do you see? Long-tail boats laden with bright blooms of colour gliding along the Chao Phraya River that leads to The Oriental, Bangkok. Frangipanis and lilies scent the tropical air beneath the blue, blue sky. You've already explored your decadent and lavishly decorated suite in this extraordinary hotel, where you follow, surrounded by over 130 years of history, in the well shod footsteps of Royalty, heads of state, and literary greats. Now is the time to make the first of many wishes come true. You board the private ferry that will carry you across the river to the traditional Thai house of carved teakwood that is the Oriental Spa. Relinquish yourself to the wellness therapists, and prepare to be enriched through the use of ancient skills and wisdom in the art of healing. Simply let go and all your extravagant wishes will come true.

Crown Towers | MELBOURNE, VICTORIA | AUSTRALIA

For your husband's 40th birthday you decided to surprise him with a weekend getaway to Melbourne, the city in which the two of you met almost ten years ago. You can not believe how much the city has changed since the two of you lived here. A friend recommended the Crown Towers and you are pleased with its desirable location, by the river at the South Bank, overlooking downtown Melbourne. You have booked one of the suites that wraps the corner of the building so that your view is both of the fabulous Yarra River and of the city itself. In the evenings, from a floor to ceiling window, the two of you watch the nightly flame show near the River before heading out for a night on the town that, once upon a time, you both called home.

KIWICOLLECTION.COM

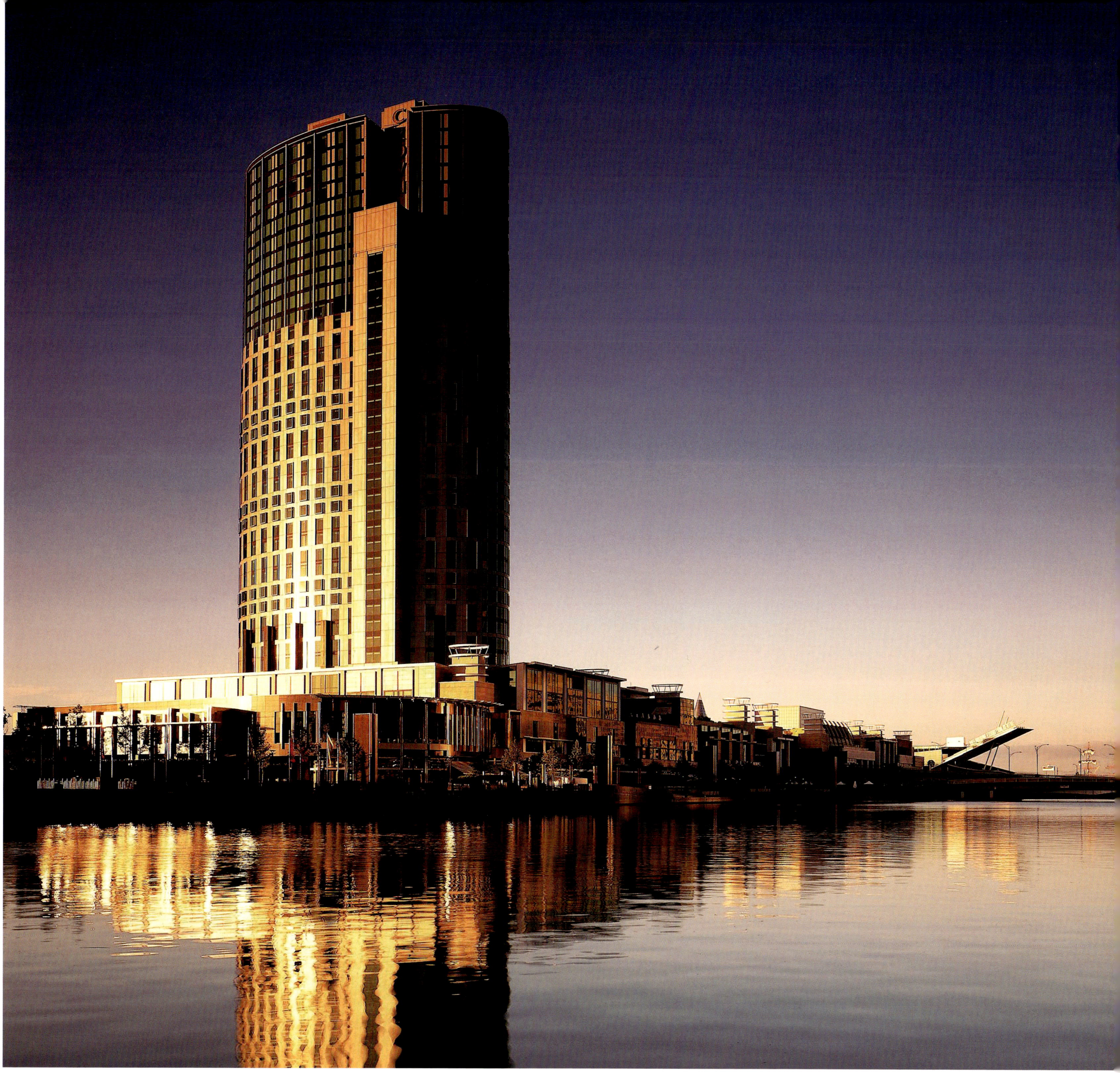

Four Seasons Hotel Singapore | SINGAPORE | SINGAPORE

Given your long standing partner status within your law firm, not to mention the tons of business you brought in last year alone, your expense account is vast; and the "Superior" and, on occasion, "Deluxe" guest room categories at the Four Seasons Hotel Singapore are for the taking. That's good, because rooms such as these serve their purpose – they are conveniently set up for work with a large writing desk, easy broadband Internet access, a king-size bed, and even in-room massage treatments available until 11PM. The hotel is just off Orchard Road, the business and entertainment Mecca of Singapore. But right now you're off to finally try to beat the tennis pro on the hotel's indoor (and thankfully air-conditioned) court.

The Spire Queenstown | QUEENSTOWN, SOUTH ISLAND | NEW ZEALAND
The subtle smell of perfume followed by the click of heels in the hallway signal that it is time to go. With a quick flick of a button the state-of-the-art 50 inch plasma screen, stone fireplace and floor lamps are extinguished. Easing out of the iconic Eames lounger, you pause to admire the alpenglow lighting up Queenstown's Southern Alps. "I absolutely love that chair," you say aloud, "I think I should get one for my study." Taking the bait she turns and says, "You do look good in that chair." "Well," you say, deliberately ensuring that you have her complete attention, "I do have a special appreciation for beautiful things…" Laughing she turns for the door, but before she has a chance to press the handle you catch her by the nook of her arm. "Beautiful things like this," you continue, presenting her with a long, slender, gold trimmed box wrapped in exquisite blue velvet. "Happy birthday, my love."

Island Shangri-La, Hong Kong | HONG KONG, S.A.R. | CHINA

As you pass through the Atrium at Island Shangri-La, admiring 'The Great Motherland of China' Chinese silk painting, you hear an echo of the turbulent days of the orient: Tai-Pans and smugglers battling over the lucrative Far East trading routes. Swords are drawn: ready to fight, manipulate, or steal, in their quest to command the magnificent financial province of Hong Kong. Today, you stride masterfully into the Harbour Room prepared to turn this meeting of traders on their heels. You will wrest control from your competitor and seize the lion's share of the market; you are the Tai-Pan. Later, you will adjourn to the Alsace Room, with several fine bottles of wine provided by the hotel's extensive wine cellar, for a private celebration of your victorious dealings. The sun eventually sets on this noteworthy day. You stare across the harbour, as your colleagues raise their glasses in a toast to your success.

The Imperial New Delhi | NEW DELHI | INDIA

Banish all thoughts of heat and dust. When the chauffeur hands you a chilled towel at the airport, you know what to expect: India at its most indulgent, the Raj at its most romantic and raffish. As the limousine glides past the royal palms and pulls up in front of the hotel's imposing façade, the promise of colonial deference is complete. The Imperial will serve your every whim, your most decadent desires. The Sikh doorman bows graciously and welcomes you to a forgotten world of riches: a world elegantly and splendidly preserved for those who wish to explore India's past. Will you have time to see more than a fraction of the 4,000 pieces of art on display? How long does it take to rediscover The Empire? So much to do, so much to savour. But first, before the adventure begins, you'll need to slip into some white flannels and contemplate history over a pink gin.

Trident Hilton, Gurgaon | GURGAON, NATIONAL CAPITAL TERRITORY OF DELHI | INDIA

A light breeze carries the scent of frangipani into your room as you sleep. Your senses stir and you open your eyes. From your bed you gaze through the double doors, which open as if to welcome the sun glistening on the reflection pool outside. It's been a long day and it's not over yet. You're to still convince your Indian counterparts to sign the contract. You welcomed the opportunity to rest before you met them for dinner but now, with your senses alive, you're ready to experience some of the finest dining that the Trident Hilton has to offer. As you walk from your suite, you admire the imposing architecture of this unique space and arrive at the restaurant feeling relaxed. You greet your counterparts and within no time at all you're talking business. Though, this time, it seemed all that was needed to convince them to sign was the incredible ambiance of the hotel, and a perfectly cold Indian beer.

CITY 175

Conrad Bangkok | BANGKOK | THAILAND

Remember that backpacking trip you took to Thailand before university? When you wanted to change the world? Hemp clothing, no make-up on the ladies, and Birkenstocks all around. And that girl Sarah (or did she rename herself Sunshine?) – didn't she have dreadlocks? Now, sitting in the lounge at the Conrad Bangkok, you're happy to have those days long behind you. This is the lifestyle you aspired to – fast paced business amidst luxurious surroundings and first class service. Still, the feeling is the same – the air outside hot and sweet, the scent of chili peppers and coriander riding on a whisper of a breeze – and you feel the same hopefulness you did on your first trip. You see a familiar face across the room. Is it actually Sarah? Definitely without dreadlocks. Definitely wearing Chanel. The two of you retire to the bar, and over martinis, reminisce. "Remember how we wanted to change the world?" you ask. "But we are," she says. "Now we actually are."

The Ritz-Carlton, Tokyo | TOKYO | JAPAN

Whenever your husband announces that he has an upcoming business trip to Tokyo you are eager to join him. So when you heard he would be speaking at a five day CEO conference at The Ritz-Carlton in Tokyo, you quickly packed your bag. There is simply no better way to enjoy the cultural diversity that is Tokyo than from The Ritz-Carlton. Perched high above, yet right in the middle of, this fast-paced entertaining city, the Hotel sits amidst the trendiest of restaurants, luxury fashion houses, and towering skyscrapers. At street level, the hustle and bustle of Asia's economic powerhouse is almost overwhelming; but bearable, when you know that by the end of the day you will be relaxing with a cocktail and viewing the city from the magnificent sky lobby on the 45th floor of your hotel.

Raffles Hotel Le Royal | PHNOM PENH | CAMBODIA

You've been sent to investigate the exclusive comings and goings at the Raffles Hotel. Sitting at the famous Elephant Bar, you can't help but admire the way the rich decor is reflected in the mysterious cross-section of guests. Colourful elephant motifs adorn the ceiling. Since 1929 writers, adventurers, billionaires, and socialites have mixed in this luxurious watering hole. The merry widow eyes the rugged adventurer at the end of the bar. Similarly, he hasn't been able to take his eyes off the fresh-faced debutante since she gracefully entered the bar on the arm of her billionaire escort. It has to be the historical ambience and chivalrous charm of the Raffles Hotel that draws you into the subtle byplay. A sultry sip of her Femme Fatale and the widow stalks her prey. Sidestepping the advance, the adventurer sips his Airavata and winks at the shy debutante, who blushes. Your pen flashes across the page as you hastily write.

Park Hyatt Saigon | HO CHI MINH CITY | VIETNAM

Inspired by the Afternoon Tea at the Park Lounge: a delicious mix of spring rolls, Vietnamese delicacies, and the more traditional pastries, you've enrolled in the Park Hyatt cooking class. Having explored Saigon on foot and by tuk tuk, you cannot wait to discover Ho Chi Minh City through its diverse culinary flavours. Eagerly, you follow the sous chef on a short trip to the local market where you select fresh authentic Vietnamese ingredients. Locals smile and banter as you learn the merits of lemongrass and bok choi. You quicken your step as you return to the hotel. Donning your apron, you embark upon a mouth-watering journey of cultural and historical discovery under the expert tutelage of the culinary team at the Park Hyatt. Upon completion, you are rewarded with a selection of dishes that satisfy your taste buds and leave you eager to attempt more of the easy to follow 'House' recipes and dishes from the complimentary Vietnamese cookbook.

Mandarin Oriental Tokyo | TOKYO | JAPAN

"O" is just a letter: a round circle. "Oh." That's a little longer: an interjection, an exclamation, a sound of pleasure when you step out of the private lift onto the 38th floor sky lobby of the Mandarin Oriental Hotel and gaze across the city of Tokyo, all the way from the Imperial Palace to Tokyo Bay. In your room, things only get better. With the same wraparound view of Tokyo city, it's a blend of Japanese aestheticism and high-end entertainment/communications technology: a 45inch HDTV, yoga mats in the linen closet, a DVD with surround sound. The bathroom is divided from the room by a sheet of glass; open the wooden blinds and the room floods with light. Time for a long soak in the marble bathtub, above which is an LCD TV. Which to watch: the view or the movies? Mount Fuji wins. "M." M is just a letter. "Mmm" is a sound of pleasure.

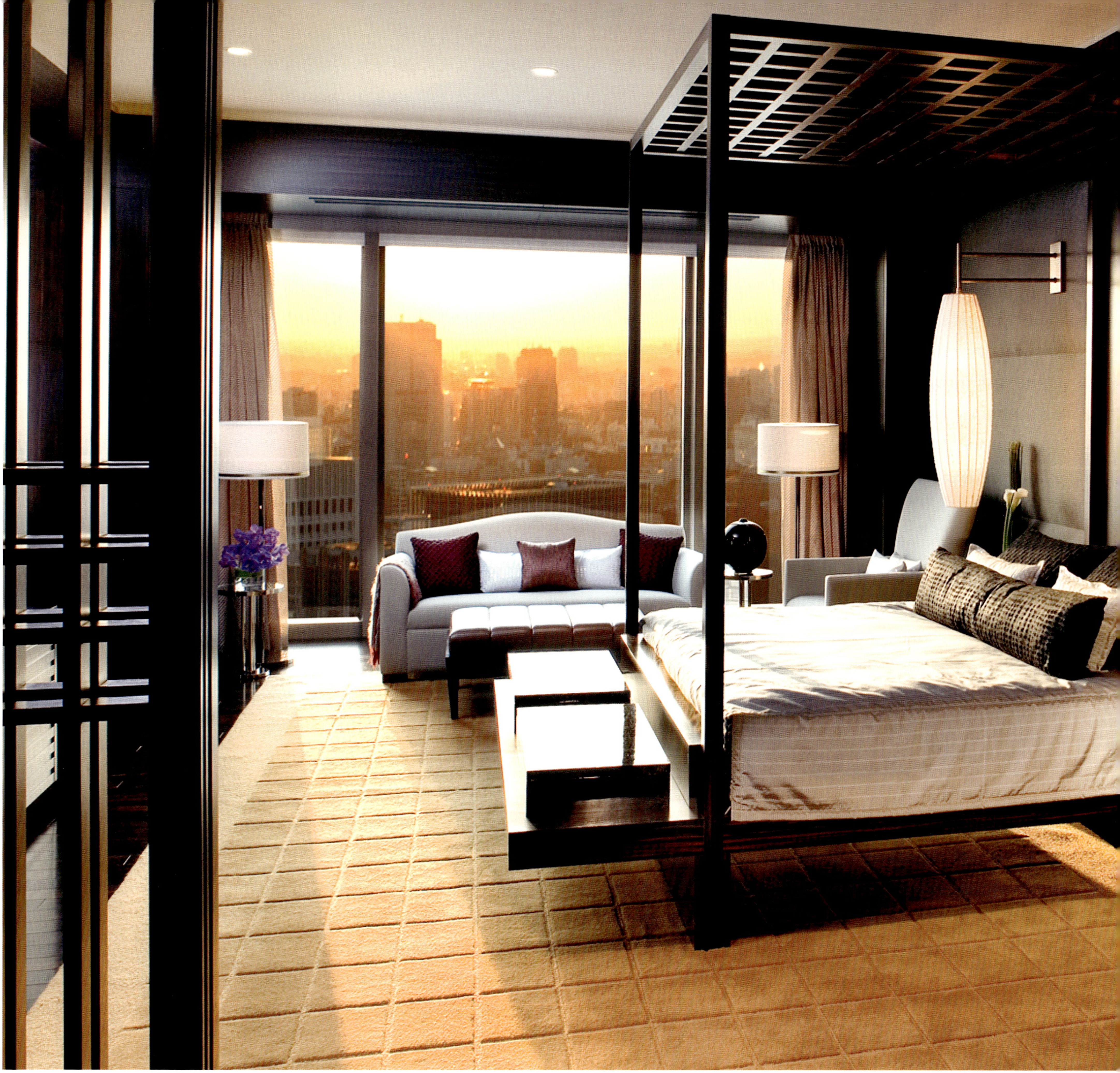

St. Regis Hotel, Beijing | BEIJING, MUNICIPALITY OF BEIJING | CHINA

Having stayed at many St. Regis hotels previously, you arrive at the St. Regis Hotel, Beijing with clear expectations. There is a level of service, décor, and enjoyment standards that you have come to expect of practically any hotel, and most certainly of a St. Regis Hotel, regardless of where you are in the world. Naturally, this one did not disappoint. Living up to its brand name, the hotel offered a fast and efficient butler on each floor, exceptional business amenities, and a bright and courteous staff who made your visit most enjoyable. And although there simply was no time to partake of the pleasure on this particular trip, you hear the hotel spa is one of the best in the entire city – good to know for the next visit.

Maison Souvannaphoum Hotel | LUANG PRABANG | LAO PDR

Last night's candle lit dinner at Elephant Blanc included a few more glasses of red wine then you had anticipated and, consequently, you lingered well into the night. So, in a moment of weakness before bed, you agreed to forsake your regular morning walk and champagne breakfast in exchange for a few extra hours of sleep. Hours later, as the pale-grey light of Luang Prabang's famous misty mornings grew brighter, you could hear that familiar sound of saffron robed monks chanting in the distance. Knowing this hotel was once the home of Laotian royalty, you could imagine the Prince and Princess Souvannaphouma lying together and listening, as you are now, to the monk's peaceful procession. Then suddenly, as if inspired by their quiet dedication, you were both up and out the door. After all, if the monks can get up for rice and bread, surely you can get up for a champagne breakfast.

Sofitel Queenstown | QUEENSTOWN, SOUTH ISLAND | NEW ZEALAND

Bill; thanks for your message. I'm sorry to hear things have been crazy in the office while I'm here in Queenstown. (Translated: Bill, if it wasn't for your message I almost would have forgotten about the office for all the fun I'm having here.) The conference has been very demanding. I've been leaving the facility late each night, not even eating an evening meal before crawling to my hotel room. (Translated: The conference has been extremely enjoyable. The Sofitel's conference and hotel facilities are exceptional and the backdrop of Queenstown's snow capped mountains is truly inspiring. Each evening, I've been dining on delectable French cuisine at Sofitel's Vie Restaurant before retiring to my room and enjoying the best night's sleep I've ever had in the plushest bed I've ever slept.) There's hardly been time for anything outside of work. (Translated: Visited vineyards, have been jet boating and bungee jumping.) See you soon. (Translated: Considering a transfer.)

The Peninsula Bangkok | BANGKOK | THAILAND

Standing on your balcony at The Peninsula Bangkok, you sip a refreshing glass of iced lemongrass tea while the maid lays out your clothes for the evening. Below you, the 'River of Kings', the Chao Phraya River reflects the rosy hues of the sky as the sun sinks behind the skyscrapers in the west. Last night, you merged with the crowds, joining families of locals as you explored the Patpong Night Market. Escaping down a narrow street, you stumbled upon an ancient Buddhist temple. Following the stone pathway and scent of sandalwood, you discovered a shrine of glowing red candles and orchids set before the goddess of fertility. Tonight, you will follow the concierge's advice and visit Brown Sugar. Allegedly the best jazz bar in Bangkok, it is renowned for its old Chicago jazz club ambience and style. Your anticipation builds. You don't want to be late to meet your friends for pre-excursion cocktails in the bar downstairs.

Hilton Sydney | SYDNEY, NEW SOUTH WALES | AUSTRALIA

Dear John: I am unsure how to tell you this. Words escape me. I know I need to say this in just the right way. I'm sorry, after this I will not accept any excuses from you. This has been the most magical anniversary celebration we have shared. Thank you for planning these amazing two nights at the Hilton Sydney. I have never been as pampered and indulged as I have been here with you, my darling. The bubbling champagne and chocolate dipped strawberries were a marvelous way to kick-off our celebration. I loved every moment of our joint spa therapy treatment and our romantic dinner at the Glass Brasserie, where you thoughtfully arranged for the chef to prepare my favourite meal. I will never forget the look in your eyes as we shared that rose petal strewn bath, the heady fragrance casting a spell over both of us. This anniversary was truly memorable. You are unforgettable…

Park Hyatt Tokyo | TOKYO | JAPAN
From the Peak Lounge you all gaze out yet again over bustling Tokyo and Mount Fuji in the distance. You just can't seem to get enough of this amazing view from the Park Hyatt Tokyo. As you are travelling with another couple that are old and dear friends, you had booked two rooms and requested that they be as close together as possible. You're in rooms adjacent to each other in a private area at the end of one of the hallways, which was ideally suited for your needs. The staff is uncompromisingly friendly, attentive, and helpful. Regretfully you only have one more day here and then it's back home to different cities for each couple. A grin works it way up the edges of your mouth as you remember all the exciting experiences of this journey, and imagine how you will all remember this last stop as a fitting end to a fantastic adventure.

KIWICOLLECTION.COM

Mandarin Oriental, Hong Kong | HONG KONG, S.A.R. | CHINA

Dear G, staying at the Mandarin Oriental is like coming jia! (That's Mandarin for home). From our suite's balcony, I've watched the lights of fleets of boats glitter in the night, and marvelled that so many people live in a delicate balance of East and West. We went sailing across Victoria Harbour today in a restored Chinese sailing junk. The sights were breathtaking, and the scents of the Orient teased our noses. I couldn't wait to return to the hotel knowing our personal butler had prepared Chinese tea and Oriental tapas. Just an afternoon snack! Tomorrow we've even booked into the Ayurvedic Treatment Room downstairs for 'his' and 'hers' Shanghainese pedicures. Sending you fu and xi, (luck and happiness); it's time for a long soak in the bath. I might just open the blinds so I can lie back and admire the city skyline. Hopefully nobody's looking!

Park Hyatt Sydney | SYDNEY, NEW SOUTH WALES | AUSTRALIA

There's something about Sydney; something irrepressible, something familiar yet stirring. You've seen it in a thousand pictures, a thousand films; but never this close, never in the flesh, never framed so vividly. At the Park Hyatt Sydney fills your dreams, your days, and even your drinks. As you sip your martini, the Opera House is reflected in the glass; as you stare lazily out of the floor to ceiling windows, your eyes irresistibly are drawn to the Harbour Bridge. From the restaurant to the bars, the rooftop terrace to your room, you're enveloped and embraced by the waterfront. Is this a boat or a building? Are you floating or on land? Perhaps you're on a luxury liner, a majestic cruise ship, your voyage about to begin. At any moment, you'll weigh anchor and glide silently and serenely into the open sea; in your wake, a city with sights you'll never forget.

Kemang Icon | JAKARTA, JAVA | INDONESIA

The moment your limousine delivered you to Kemang Icon, you knew this experience would be special. The smiling staff welcomed you by name and escorted you through an arcade of elegant boutiques before whizzing you upwards, in the glass lift, to a lobby that resembled a stylish bar. Entering your room, you were greeted with the soothing scent of burning oils, per your specifications, and bath toiletries tailored to suit your personal and aroma-therapeutic needs. Every little detail necessary to make your stay in this hidden sanctuary, amidst the exuberant bustle of Jakarta, a unique experience has been met. Now you must decide between a relaxing Indonesian therapy at Mybodyspa or an afternoon spent beneath the high ceilings of your room, where the latest in technology is available for your entertainment and enjoyment. If you're really good, you may just get some work done before it's time for another evening meal of sumptuous dishes with flashes of Indonesian spice.

The Ritz-Carlton, Millenia Singapore | SINGAPORE | SINGAPORE

Tomorrow's activity, if you can call it an activity, is to eat your way through Singapore. The goal: sample as many different tastes of Asian cuisine as is physically possible in one day. You long have heard that Singapore is famous for its street food, but have yet to experience this first hand. There are plenty of formal restaurants in and around your hotel, The Ritz-Carlton, Millenia Singapore (many of which you have visited more than once) but, tomorrow, you will be seeking solely Singapore street food. And it looks to be not just a gastronomic, but also a cultural experience – Malaysian, Indian, and Cantonese cuisines served Pacific Rim fusion style. And Singapore being as immaculately clean as it is, you know that street vendors are likely to adhere to more stringent health standards than some of the better restaurants back home.

Hiiragiya | KYOTO | JAPAN
Your husband has surprised you for your birthday with a gift of a weekend in Kyoto. Knowing how much you love the Japanese refined culture and attention to even the minutest of details, he has reserved a room at the Hiiragiya-Ryokan. The rooms are of the traditional Japanese guest room ilk, exquisitely and uniquely decorated - each with a charm and mystique of its own. For dinner, in celebration of yet another birthday (where does the time go?) you dine in-house, savouring the fine quality Kaiseki cuisine, prepared with finesse using the season's freshest ingredients and served on elegant lacquer ware and Kyoto-crafted ceramics. Tomorrow, you will be treated to a day of shopping in the trendy boutique stores of Kyoto. Maybe another birthday isn't going to be so bad, after all.

The Regency at The Galle Face Hotel | COLOMBO | SRI LANKA

People call you crazy. But, you don't listen to what others say. You simply like to think of yourself as passionate. There is no doubt that indulging in your passions is made easy when staying at The Regency at The Galle Face Hotel. You're passionate about sport. You've spent the last few days with your closest friends enjoying the excitement of a scintillatingly close cricket match in Colombo. You're passionate about food and wine. Over the past week you've indulged in many fine bottles of vintage wine and champagne from the hotel's cellar and are now delighted by the thought of choosing one of the hotel's nine superb eateries for dinner. You're passionate in your pursuit of perfection. The inescapable sunsets, the service, and the superb surrounds of the hotel all indulge this pursuit. You realise that you may be crazy if you ever leave this place. There could be some truth in what people say, after all.

The Oberoi Amarvilâs, Agra | AGRA, UTTAR PRADESH | INDIA

From the balcony of your suite at The Oberoi Amarvilâs it feels as if you can reach out and almost touch the magnificent dome of the Taj Mahal. You feel the apricot and peach bands of the sunset, the lilac and lavender tones of the twilight that frame the monument to eternal love. The breeze rustles the pages of a scarred diary flipping to an entry you made fifty years earlier in this city. Once before you stood together watching the sunset, arms wrapped around one another's waists, awestruck by the magnificence of man and his power to feel. You have returned to Agra to rediscover the former Mughal kingdom, to explore the old marketplace of the Kinari Bazaar and indulge in your rose hued memories. You listen as the butler finishes drawing your bath. You are eager to finish watching the sun disappear from the soothing liquid warmth of your freestanding bathtub.

KIWICOLLECTION.COM

Wynn Macau | MACAU, S.A.R. | CHINA

"Welcome to the Vegas of the Orient." The pilot's voice echoes through your headphones as the helicopter drops towards the iconic Wynn Macau. A cascade of water shoots up from the man-made lake, catching the light like millions of sparkling diamonds. You have arrived. Everything you need is here in this fantastical world; gilded in gold, accented in red, and adorned with the finest of Swarovski crystal. The porter disappears with your luggage. You rise towards the sky once again, destination the casino. Your playground awaits. Cards snap together, before landing softly on green velvet, as the croupier deals the deck. Chips click beneath your fingers as you watch the game of chance unfold before you. You tap the table-top. The croupier hits you with one more card. Silence. You wink and turn over your cards. Blackjack! Luck is with you tonight. Next the roulette wheel, and later, a high stakes poker game. This is living.

The Ritz-Carlton, Osaka | OSAKA-SHI | JAPAN

You admire the views of downtown Osaka from your traditional Japanese style suite at The Ritz-Carlton. Tonight, you have invited a select group of friends to join you for an evening of sake tasting; sake served with all the tradition and ceremony inherent to the rich culture of Japan. The sake sommelier places the last of the glazed ceramic beverage ware on the low table in the reception room. A footbath sits by a neat row of black slippers at the base of the shohji screen. Once you all are seated on cushions around the low table, the sommelier begins your introduction to the flavoursome fermented rice beverage native to Japan. As the evening concludes, you raise your cup of Junmaishu grade sake to the ceiling in a final toast. "Kampai!" You register the mellow bouquet first, then the rich smooth flavour of the sake as it slides along your tongue.

KIWICOLLECTION.COM

88 Xintiandi | SHANGHAI, MUNICIPALITY OF SHANGHAI | CHINA

Putting down your copy of the 'Joy Luck Club', you step out onto the balcony of your stylishly modern suite at 88 Xintiandi. A candlelit table for two, dressed in white linen and silver cutlery, waits patiently, the air fragrant with orange blossom and spice. The city of Shanghai is laid out in all its panoramic glory before you. The juxtaposition of the ancient mysteries of the Orient and the chic modern energy of a metropolis is a refreshing surprise to your trip. You hear the outer door to the suite open and close, followed by the soft thud of a briefcase dropping to the carpeted floor. A shiver of anticipation tingles along your skin. You can't wait to share with your partner tales of the day's adventures exploring this city. Your eyes sparkle in the moonlight, reflecting off the lake beside the hotel, as you turn to re-enter the suite. This evening is lush with the promise of mysterious pleasures.

Park Hyatt Seoul | SEOUL | SOUTH KOREA

Surely you're in the wrong place. There's been some confusion, an embarrassing mix-up, and you've taken someone else's room. In fact, it's not a room at all: it's a luxury apartment. You ring reception to explain the mistake. But there's no error. "The Park Hyatt has the largest guest rooms in the city," says the girl reassuringly. "We call them 'residence rooms', because they're more like apartments." Indeed they are. As you stare out of the window, the city spread out below, you realise that you're staying in a penthouse suite. Everything about the room is big, from the king-size bed to the granite bathtub, from the television screen to the dining table. Then you remember the lobby. Perhaps it's not such a surprise after all. Any hotel that puts its lobby on the top floor, to benefit from far-reaching views, is committed to dimensions. And when it comes to time and space, right now, there's nowhere you'd rather be.

Conrad Tokyo | TOKYO | JAPAN

It's hard to find fault with the Conrad Tokyo. You know a number of people who have stayed in Tokyo and all say that the Conrad is an unexpectedly cool and trendy business hotel. Location-wise it is well positioned – an hour from the airport and near the underground system so that you can get anywhere you need to be quickly and easily. But the rooms are what make the hotel so spectacular. The mahogany wood accents, glass, Asian-style bed and seating, flatscreen TV, and electronic controls for lighting and window blinds (including the bathroom glass wall divider to living area) create a perfect blend of modern, sleek, and comfortable. Small touches here and there show that this hotel cares about its guest: a single orchid floating in a water vase in the entry, bottled water, fresh kiwi with napkin, plate and knife, a rubber ducky at the tub, a cute tiny teddy bear at bed turn-down in the evening, great Shisheido toiletries, and, of course, the heated Toto toilet.

CASA Colombo | COLOMBO | SRI LANKA

You begin the over well turning over the strike; it's necessary if you're going to reach the competitive total set by the county team here at the historical cricket grounds in Colombo. The bowler runs in and your partner dollies the ball back for a caught and bowled. Wicket! You square up at the crease; all hope of victory lies with you. Eye on the ball, you swing, connecting willow with leather; the ball smashes over the boundary. Six! You raise your bat high, that's your century and that's the game. From the rear seat of your CASA Domo driven vintage car, you sip champagne as the lights of the city flash by. Back at the two hundred year old Moorish mansion some call CASA, but you refer to as your home away from home, you open with a toast to your worthy opponents. In the hip surrounds of the open-air Za-Za restaurant the celebrations will rage till dawn.

The Eugenia | BANGKOK | THAILAND

You roar up the ornate drive to the 19th century colonial style house that is The Eugenia, a quite luxurious oasis in the heart of Bangkok, in a lovingly maintained vintage Jaguar MK VII. The breeze whispers of the glorious days of Far East history. Glancing at your watch you grin. Perfect. You are just in time for evening cocktails and canapés in the hotel's Zhang He Lounge. Inside, your fellow guests have already gathered to enjoy the pre-dinner refreshments; invariably talk turns to the lounge's namesake. An intrepid explorer and adventurer, Admiral Zhang He, is reputed to have sailed the largest fleet of junks from China across South-East Asia to Persia and on to Africa. As the conversation ensues you sit back in the comfortable antique armchair and sip your aperitif, content to let the chatter flow around you.

KIWICOLLECTION.COM

Four Seasons Hotel Hong Kong | HONG KONG, S.A.R. | CHINA

Your experience today leaves no doubt that the shopping in Hong Kong rivals that of any city in the world. Your arms laden with shopping bags, you step into the foyer of the Four Seasons Hotel Hong Kong and are immediately met by the concierge who helps the bags from your arms. Exhausted after a day of shopping, you slowly make your way to your suite, contemplating an evening of room service - French cuisine from the hotel's Caprice restaurant - and a long hot bath. Opening the door to your room, you notice that the concierge has placed your shopping bags neatly on your bed. However, it is the incredible vista of Victoria Harbour that truly strikes you. The lights of the city brilliantly contrast with the night sky. The city feels alive. At once, you feel re-energised. The nightlife in Hong Kong beckons. As you rifle through today's purchases you realise that your only dilemma now is deciding which dress to wear.

The Observatory Hotel | SYDNEY, NEW SOUTH WALES | AUSTRALIA

Make me a star, your sweetheart whispers. As an independant film director, you're used to fulfilling this request. Thing is, you've got business to take care of in Sydney. So you book a room at The Observatory Hotel. You handle a potential merger while your loved one explores the city. At the end of the day, you meet over an eight-course dinner. Afterward, the two of you have a swim in the indoor pool, its domed ceiling resembling a Southern Hemisphere sky full of stars. You are inspired. You grasp your partner's hand. "Let's go," you say. You head off for the Sydney Observatory. Heady with wine, you pick out a star, a brilliant fixture in the heavens. You name it after your beloved. Can the night get any better? It can. It will. The stars never shone so brightly.

Les Suites Taipei Ching-Cheng | TAIPEI | TAIWAN

Over the last two weeks, Les Suites has been your personal oasis of contemporary style and elegance in a city filled with huge grey monoliths. And now, after a day of high-energy presentations and hard-line negotiations in a brightly lit office in one of those massive towers, you cannot wait to return to the chic, champagne club-like setting of your hotel. As the elevator descends, you can almost taste that gin martini on your lips. You can feel the tension in your forehead soften just thinking about the subdued lighting and gentle jazz that will be playing in your suite. And that shower. You cannot wait to stand in that incredible glass enclosed stall and let that enormous downpour rain-shower head rinse the strain of the day away before you head out on the town for supper. So far, the manager's recommendations have been superb and you wonder what gem he'll uncover for you tonight.

The Landmark Mandarin Oriental | HONG KONG, S.A.R. | CHINA

Dear M: The children are enjoying themselves immensely here at The Landmark Mandarin Oriental in Hong Kong. Enjoyment began for them with the customised welcome gifts they received upon arrival. The thoughtful hotel included kid's size bathrobes for both. For Tommy there was the added surprise of a sketchbook and crayons; you know how he loves to draw. For Annabelle, her favourite scented bath products which she delights in at bath time. I've dropped them off for a special children's yoga class where the instructor challenges them to hold positions like the elephant and the fish. This provides the perfect opportunity for me to dash across to the Landmark Atrium for some retail therapy and, as well, indulge my passion for elegant designs and rich fabrics. The concierge has arranged for us to visit Hong Kong's Zoological and Botanical Gardens tomorrow; the children are especially excited to see the Jaguar Enclosure. Don't worry, I'll pick out something exceptional for you too…

Hotel Maya | KUALA LUMPUR | MALAYSIA

Business has brought you back to Kuala Lumpur. But this time, you thought you'd take the advice of your overworked assistant and stay somewhere different. Sensing your initial reluctance, your assistant assured you that the hotel is centrally located – only eight minutes walk from the Petronas Towers. You agreed, considering that you usually spend very little time in your hotel room anyway. However, now here at Hotel Maya, you are overwhelmed by your desire to experience everything that the hotel has to offer. You're not sure whether it's the hydrotherapy pool, your daily massages at the Anggun spa, or the organic food from the Anggun Café that has left you feeling so relaxed. You experience such delight in feeling so good that when your assistant calls, you advise everyone to take the rest of the day off. You can do nothing but smile when you overhear your assistant whisper to another colleague, "Mission accomplished".

lebua at State Tower | BANGKOK | THAILAND

His demeanor is friendly, yet focused. His movements are both fluid and deliberate. The speed and precision with which he handles his razor sharp Santoku knife is absolutely astonishing. You've watched talented chefs at work before but never in a setting as intimate as your own suite – a necessity on this occasion since even you couldn't crash the three month waiting list at the roof-top Breeze restaurant with such short notice. Part of you feels guilty for neglecting your guests but you've become intoxicated with the edgy aromas and unique concoctions of the east meets west fare, and enthralled by the chef's penchant for showmanship. Stepping back from the counter he smiles, clasps his hands, and bows ever so slightly. Dinner is ready. You turn to your guests and gesture towards the dining room table.

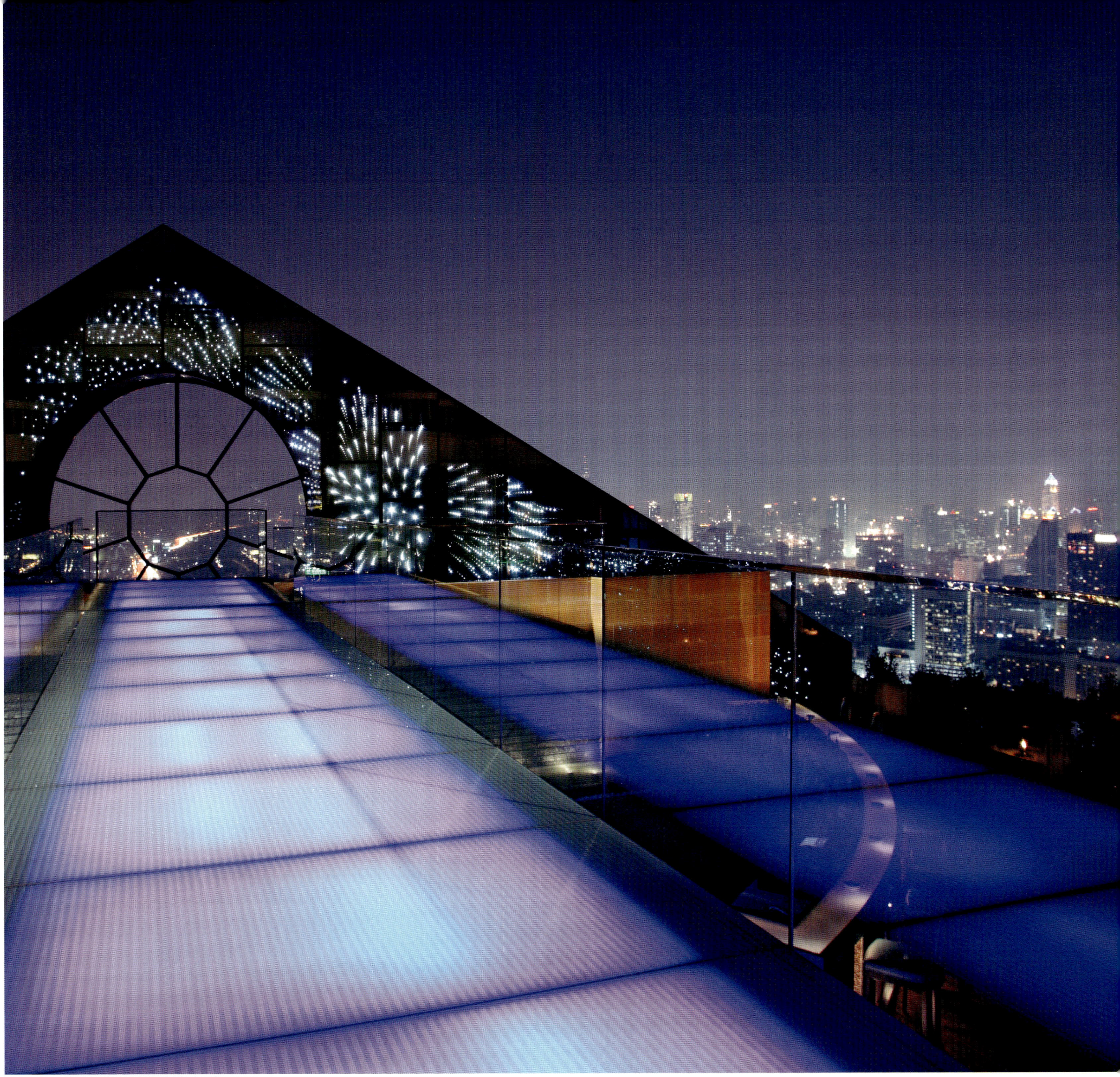

Four Seasons Hotel Shanghai | SHANGHAI, MUNICIPALITY OF SHANGHAI | CHINA

Shanghai was a novelty the first couple of times you came here on business, but now suddenly everything seems claustrophobic: the glass and concrete high-rises, the chaotic crowds, the insane traffic. Three days of hectic business meetings in the city have left you on edge, so you escape to the Four Seasons, situated on Nanjing Road away from the crowds. At the hotel, a two-hour Balinese massage and four-course dinner are in order. A business associate calls to set up a meeting for the following day. Deep breath. "Fine," you say, "but let's meet at Si Ji Jiu Dian (Chinese for the Four Seasons)." A call to the concierge ensues. The hotel will get you a boardroom for two, arrange a translator, and make sure your suit is pressed for the next day. Done like dinner. This is one meeting you won't be dreading.

Grand Hyatt Tokyo | TOKYO | JAPAN

Time is your enemy. You have one weekend to experience the splendours of the Grand Hyatt: a mere 48 hours to explore the endless possibilities for dining, entertainment, and recreation. Where do you begin? You're like a child in a theme park: not a minute to waste, not a second to squander. First stop, the Maduro. How quaintly Japanese, you think, as you enter the bar by crossing a bridge over a pond. Next, after a quick sake, you relax on the open-air terrace of the Fiorentina Café and order the finest Italian cuisine. But the clock is ticking. How will you ever sample all the hotel's eating places and bars? And what about the spa and fitness club? The waiter reads your thoughts and smiles sympathetically. Yes, he knows the frustrations. So much to enjoy, so much to savour, but so little time. The decision is simple: you'll have to come back. For a week or two.

Banyan Tree Bangkok | BANGKOK | THAILAND

Meet me on top of the world, the note read. Excited, you step from the lift and discover the city, in all its glittering neon lit glory, laid at your feet. 61 floors high, you are left breathless by the open-air rooftop lounge at Banyan Tree Bangkok, with its wooden decks, muted lighting, and amazing views. A waiter presents you with a fizzing glass of champagne and a note folded neatly on a silver tray. Walk amongst the clouds with me. Sighing, you cannot refuse. You follow the waiter down wooden steps to your own private romantic dining deck; candles flicker on the white tabletop and bottles of champagne rest on ice. The waiter disappears. No more notes – no more mystery. It's just the two of you and the view across the table is as stunning as any you'll see up here.

The Portman Ritz-Carlton, Shanghai | SHANGHAI, MUNICIPALITY OF SHANGHAI | CHINA

Ripples of water caress your skin as you turn effortlessly and begin another lap in the indoor pool at The Portman Ritz-Carlton. The cobalt blue of the water shimmers in the white surrounds of the grand room. Seated on a pool lounger, your partner excitedly sorts through a myriad of 'logoed' bags from your shopping expedition along Nanjing Road, just one of the many fabulous streets in Shanghai, the 'Paris of the Orient'. Rich silks, their bright colours luminescent, catch the light reflecting off the pool as your partner blows you a kiss. As you make a final turn, a waiter discreetly glides along the poolside carrying twin tumblers of amber liquid over ice. One more lap to go and you can join your partner in a nightcap before you both retire to the comfortable elegance of your suite upstairs.

The Henry Jones Art Hotel | HOBART, TASMANIA | AUSTRALIA

You follow the bellman through the foyer of The Henry Jones Art Hotel to your room. The original timber beams of the converted waterfront warehouse and jam factory have been worn smooth over the years. Framed works of artistic photographers give way to original pieces of machinery from the historic jam factory. A charcoal portrait captures your attention. The graceful lines and soulful expression of the subject are thought provoking; what had caused that melancholy look in those big eyes? The bellman coughs to regain your attention and you move away from the portrait. The visual art is repeated inside your suite, complementing the natural timber furnishings and exotic silk adornments. Before the bellman leaves, he opens the curtains revealing another spectacular piece of visual art. Below, two fishing trawlers slip from their harbour berths in pursuit of tomorrow morning's catch, deep blue waters rippling against their bows as the sun streams through the clouds.

New Majestic Hotel | SINGAPORE | SINGAPORE

Dear G: You were right to suggest a break following the successful completion of that business project. This trip to the New Majestic Hotel, in the historic Chinatown district of the exciting city of Singapore, has been more than just a well-earned reward. Frankly, it's been a revelation. The hotel combines chic modern art with the rich traditions of the area, to create a masterpiece of comfort and style that is inspiring. I'm happy with my choice of the Loft Room, where sleeping has taken on a wonderful new dimension. The bedchamber rests on columns, high in the attic space. Here, sleeping is like floating in the air on a cloud of luxuriously soft down and feathers wrapped in the purest of cottons. Each morning, I awake refreshed and eager to discover more of the hidden mysteries of this unique destination.

Iori | KYOTO | JAPAN

"How would you describe your ryokan experience?" "Simply fantastic!" You were at Iori, a traditional tatami style ryokan in historic Kyoto, for a short break during a hectic business trip to Tokyo. Nestled deep in the surrounding neighbourhood it was an ideal location for access to the famous temples, shrines and local restaurants. While maintaining the old character of the house, Iori has integrated all the modern comforts you greatly appreciated, even providing a Nakashima chair in which you spent several relaxing hours. The traditional Byobu screen, old ceramic pot and hanging scroll gave a very authentic feel to the room. Returning from an enjoyable dinner at a nearby restaurant one evening, you had quietly 'snuck' back into the house, trying to make as little noise as possible, and feeling that you really were at 'home' for the night. "So, when are you going back?" "As soon as possible!"

Hyatt Hotel Canberra - A Park Hyatt Hotel | CANBERRA | AUSTRALIA

Sometimes everything just comes together, and this past week was one of those times. Your wedding anniversary just happens to coincide with a business trip to Canberra, which just happens to fall on Australia Day. So you decide to treat yourselves to a weekend at the Hyatt Hotel Canberra. What a charming and romantic hotel! Because it is a business trip you stay in a Club Deluxe King Room with access to the Ambassador Lounge, an enormous room with plenty of space to move and every comfort provided. And because it is your anniversary, you are happy to walk, hand in hand, through the beautiful green city of Canberra, dining at a quaint (read: dark and romantic) Italian restaurant and taking in a relaxing nightcap at the hotel.

The Leela Palace Kempinski Bangalore | BANGALORE, KARNATAKA | INDIA
Bits and bytes, 1s, and 0s, mega-this, giga-that – Ack! Right now you just want to turn your entire brain into one of the 0s, as in OFF. Bangalore certainly is one of the IT hubs of the world, and if it wasn't for the enormous opportunities available here it's unlikely that you would have found a reason to come. But now you're here, and there's no option but to forge ahead and get the contract settled. At least you've found the ultimate sanctuary from all the chaos, here at The Leela Palace Kempinski Bangalore. Ah yes, sanctuary – that's the perfect word, you think, as you head off for your daily visit to the spa. Perhaps you won't turn off your entire brain just yet. After all, how else would you so thoroughly enjoy the pleasures of that great technological innovation, the hydrotherapy room.

KIWICOLLECTION.COM

CITY 217

JUNGLE

Four Seasons Tented Camp Golden Triangle, Thailand | CHIANG RAI | THAILAND
The Four Seasons Tented Camp is reminiscent of an episode of Fantasy Island. From the moment you stepped off the plane in Chiang Rai, till you sadly boarded the outboard skiff to return down the Mekong from whence you came, you were completely blown away by this fantasy jungle experience. To call this just a 'hotel' or 'resort' is really to miss the point altogether. Imagine staying in the most authentic, luxurious, and hospitable lodge right smack in the middle of a jungle. Imagine being hands-on trained to drive and trek your own elephant through Thailand's tropical jungles and mountain trails. Sure, the elephant is known in these parts as the "gentle giant", but one look at this animal and you remember it is a giant, nonetheless, and certainly a force with which to be reckoned.

KIWICOLLECTION.COM

JUNGLE 221

KIWICOLLECTION.COM

Mahua Kothi | BANDHAVGARH NATIONAL PARK, MADHYA PRADESH | INDIA
As a well-seasoned safari traveller, you have eagerly awaited the opening Mahua Kothi, Madhya Pradesh's first luxury lodge. Although your frequent expeditions into the various wildlife preserves of Africa to track the Big Five have been well worth the time and expense (and have resulted in spectacular wildlife pictures and memories), you have seen the animals you wanted to see and are ready for new terrain - India. Rumor has it that only India delivers the tiger, and the expeditions folded into a stay at Mahua Kothi are reputed to be more discreet and nuanced than the traditional African safari. And so, here you are, full of anticipation and ready to be one of the first to find out if all the buzz about the Indian safari is true.

Raffles Grand Hotel d'Angkor | SIEM REAP | CAMBODIA

Staff at Raffles didn't flinch when you wanted to host a get-together of your college alumni group. As history and culture buffs, you're here to explore the Angkor Temples. Your group has tastes that run to the formal and traditional, which is why you've chosen Raffles – they handle every request with grace and decorum, and the rooms are tastefully appointed with art deco, country-style furnishings, and Cambodian objects d'art. Your group spends the day at the Temples, and you marvel at the walled and moated royal city of Angkor Thom, the floating village of Tonle Sap Lake. At day's end, everyone is exhausted (including, thankfully, that boorish fellow who can never keep his trap shut). Some opt for a massage, others for the hydrotherapy room. Afterwards, you congregate in the gardens for much-needed gin and tonics. Should you spend the next day exploring more temples? "No," says one of your colleagues. "The culture here suits me just fine."

KIWICOLLECTION.COM

Maya Ubud Resort & Spa | UBUD, BALI | INDONESIA

You checked into the jungle hideaway of Maya Ubud last week, determined to finish that work project away from the distractions of the office. You already have extended your stay once as the project deadline draws imminent. Yesterday, you were lured from your desk deep into the tropical rainforest. The call of native birds beckoned you along the bush track and delivered you into the cultural delights of Ubud village. The day before that, your computer sat idly as you plunged down the river and bounced along on a white water rafting adventure. Today, you float suspended amongst the trees in your private infinity edge pool. Your laptop beeps ominously from the terrace beside the pool. It's a request for the project manager. Oops! That's you. Fingers fly across the keyboard and you click 'send'. Good thing you completed that project days ago, now you can focus on the important business of floating in silky waters overlooking the river valley.

Ubud Hanging Gardens | UBUD, BALI | INDONESIA

Cobalt blue sky above, verdant green rice fields below. You float suspended amongst the trees, the terrace villa hovers above the ridge. The funicular carries you all the way to your honeymoon destination. Tropical blooms in every colour decorate the Balinese style villa. The king-size bed is scattered with orchids and frangipanis, the sheer white drapes, tied back, allow a clear view of the infinity edge pool just beyond the bedroom windows. With a chuckle, your partner draws you down to the bed; the flowers crushed beneath you offer a small perfumed protest. Tomorrow, as the morning mist slowly dissolves in the balmy tropical air, you'll ride the funicular to the bottom of the valley. Along the riverbank where the water sings as it flows over the rocks, you will be indulged in a specially designed holistic experience at Ayung Spa. That's tomorrow. Now it's just the two of you and the crushed petals.

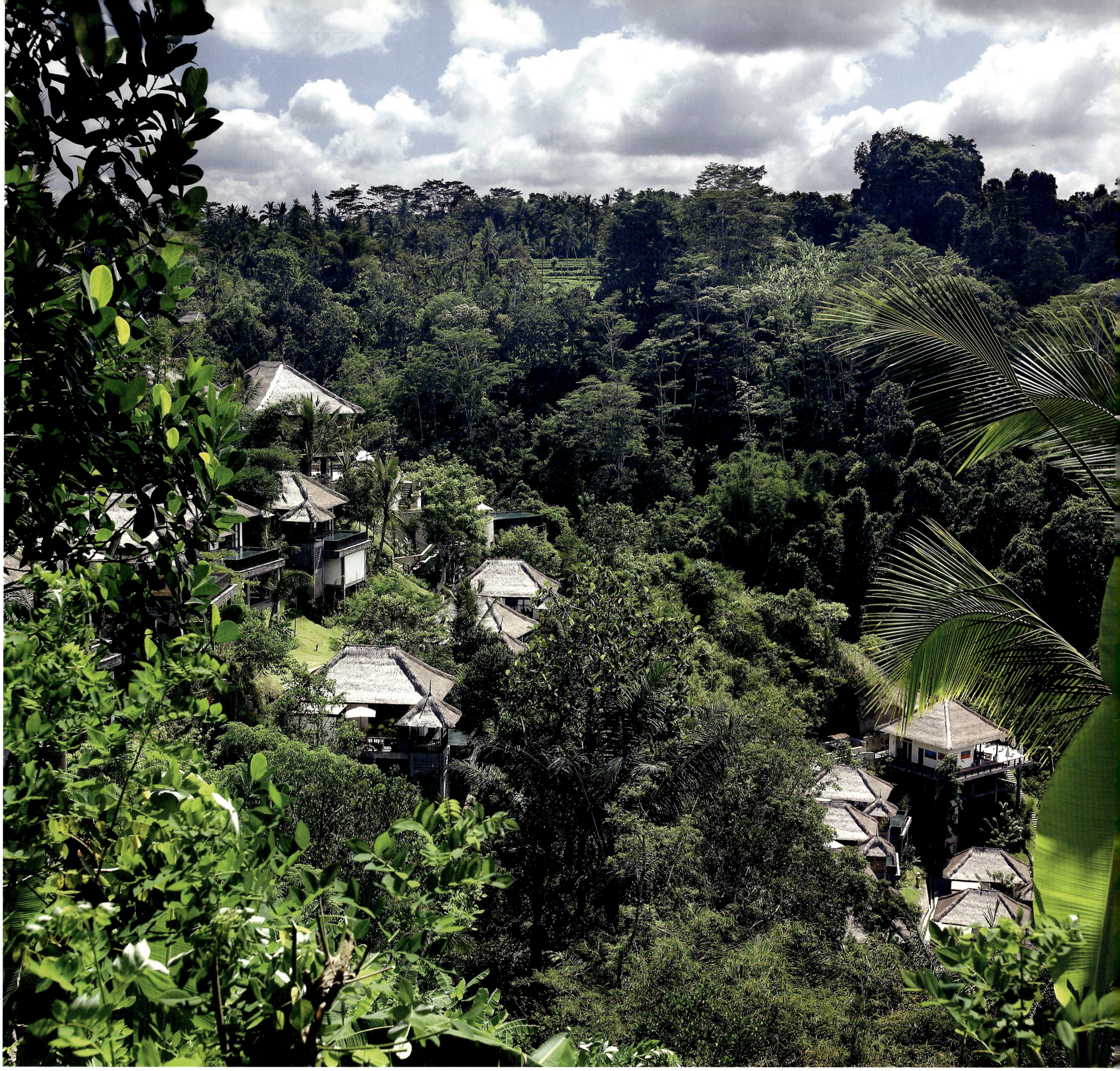

La Résidence Phou Vao | LUANG PRABANG | LAO PDR

A old wooden barge heads down the Mekong River, not too fast and not too slow. It's a basic boat with padded wooden benches and wicker chairs. You and a couple dozen other passengers silently are enjoying the ride down the Mekong, one of the longest rivers in the world. Snaking through the verdant jungle, the barge arrives at its destination: La Résidence Phou Vao. Your destination. The hotel overlooks the remote and peaceful town of Luang Prabang. Bougainvillea, palms, and frangipani flourish. Doors of passages are painted with guardian divinities. And from your room, decorated with rosewood furniture and adorned with soft cotton fabrics, you ponder the golden glints of pagoda rooftops that pepper the distant hills. The rest of the trip is yet to come: the caves of Pak Ou, the shimmering Wat Sen temples, the spice stalls and noodle kitchens of the night markets. Smiling, you anticipate the treasures that await.

Hotel de la Paix | SIEM REAP | CAMBODIA

You lounge on a daybed, suspended on the garden veranda, overlooking the delicately landscaped courtyard at Hotel de la Paix. White pebbles border the square pond where frangipani trees in each corner scent the air - stepping stones lead to the island at its centre. Lanterns flicker; candlelight illuminating the handcrafted rich wood furnishings of your surrounds. The waiter places a side table on the daybed; the appetizing aroma of sizzling duck, fresh watermelon, and fragrant coriander teases your nose. You reach for your chopsticks and lift a delicious morsel to your mouth, delighting in the flavors that burst upon your tongue. Your guide at Angkor Wat had praised this food combination and, with every bite, your appreciation grows. As night descends on this reverent wild country its cultural treasures slumber once again, until dawn draws new awe inspired faces to its mythical steps.

Anantara Resort Golden Triangle | CHIANG RAI | THAILAND

The curling grey tail of the lead elephant disappears around a bend in the rainforest path. Lawann, the noble lady giant of the jungle, gracefully steps; securely perched on her saddle, you sway with the elephant beneath you and then come to a halt. Is that a gleam in those mysterious dark eyes as she flutters her long eyelashes at you? That is a coquettish look she slides your way. Trunk swinging, Lawann winks at you as she elegantly drops her head into the leafy foliage beside the path. Her long trunk disappears, the sound of rustling joining the cries of the native birds, as she searches out a succulent vegetarian snack. Lawann is a very cheeky elephant, you later explain to your fellow swimmers, as you float lazily in the Anantara Resort Golden Triangle infinity edge pool that looks out over the Mekhong River and across the rolling hills of Laos and Myanamar.

JUNGLE 231

The Villas at Sunway Resort Hotel & Spa | PETALING JAYA | MALAYSIA

You light your cigar and pick up your glass of wine. Your favourite CD plays softly on the sound system. Only minutes from the exuberance of Kuala Lumpur you've discovered The Villas at Sunway Resort, a welcoming retreat for the senses. Stepping outside to watch the sunset from your private terrace, the earthy aroma of the verdant tropical rainforest of your jungle getaway mingles with the smoke from your cigar. Kicking off your shoes you dangle your feet in the infinty edge plunge pool, and lean back on your elbows to watch nature's masterpiece unfold on the canvas overhead. Sweeping strokes of pinks and mauves are accented with splashes of crimson and yellow as the sky gradually darkens into a velvet blue blanket studded with sparkling stars. A slow thoughtful sip of your wine and you feel your shoulders relaxing as your soul echoes the harmony of your surroundings.

Four Seasons Resort Bali at Sayan | UBUD, BALI | INDONESIA

You are lying on a teak lounger by the pool, absent-mindedly rolling the new ring on your left hand back and forth with your thumb. You smile at your spouse, lying next to you, and looking far more relaxed and serene than he has in days. Neither of you can believe that it is all finally over, or that it went so smoothly. What is that they say about weddings – "something always goes wrong"? Well not this one, not this time. Every last detail was exactly as you had anticipated it would be. Even your new mother-in-law seemed pleased. You can't resist reliving the ceremony in your mind – the two of you standing nervously on a teak wooden deck surrounded by a huge lotus pond - while your guests gazed at the magnificent view of the Ayung Valley beyond.

Uma Ubud | UBUD, BALI | INDONESIA

Your husband and you ended your honeymoon at Uma Ubud; you wanted to save the best for last, and you were not disappointed. You stayed in one of the pool villas overlooking the amazing river canyon. The villa was spotless and huge: bedroom adorned with a great four-poster canopy bed, living room, dining room, extra large bathroom (with the best shower pressure), and comfy chairs on the porch for late night star gazing. The hotel offered a shuttle into town (a five to ten minute ride) if you wished a day of shopping and strolling. And what a gem Ubud turned out to be: great stores, art galleries, and unique dance performances. Later on in the day, you took the rice paddy walk through the almost completely flat hotel grounds. Your tour guide was very knowledgeable about farming practices and local culture, bringing yet another element to a great vacation.

La Résidence d'Angkor | SIEM REAP | CAMBODIA

Within the comfort and seclusion of your room you indulge your body and spirit with a relaxing spa treatment. Before you venture out to visit famous Angkor Wat, you've selected the Tropical Well Being package to assist you on your journey of rejuvenation at La Résidence. The scents of lemongrass, cinnamon, kaffir lime, and ginger blend in a steamy halo as you immerse yourself in the warm herbal bath. Already your muscles are beginning to unwind. Out on the terrace the Spa technician is preparing for your Tropical Massage, where Indian Ayurvedic stretching techniques will be employed, with a traditional Chinese focus on pressure points, to gently stretch your body and clear energy channels. Rejuvenated and refreshed, you feel well prepared for today's visit to the temples, and the hot air balloon flight scheduled for early tomorrow morning over the entire region.

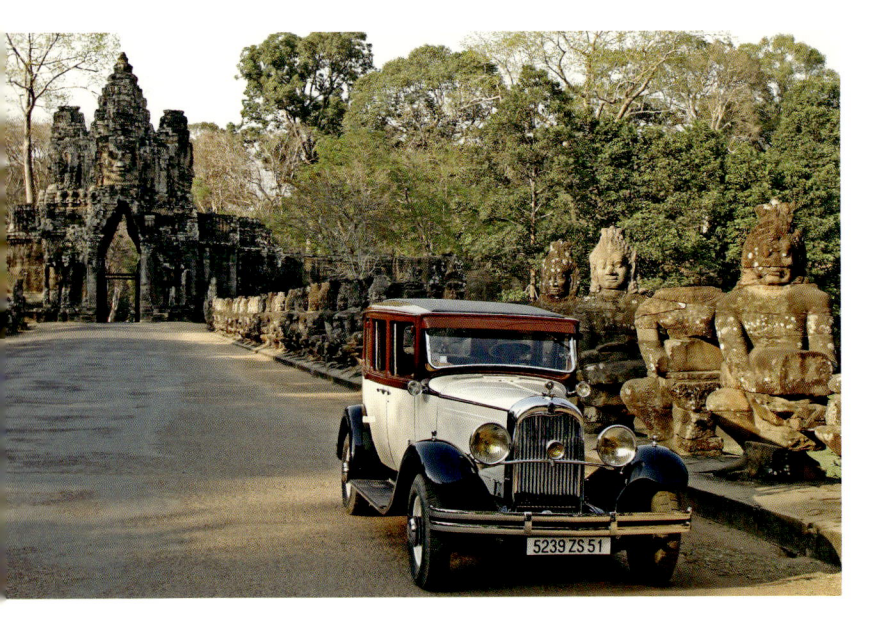

Victoria Angkor Resort & Spa | SIEM REAP | CAMBODIA

You knew travelling through Cambodia would be like stepping into a time machine. You had heard about the quiet modesty and kindness of the Kampucheans. You were prepared to delight in the pristine examples of French Colonial architecture. And, you expected to be overwhelmed by the ancient majesty of The Angkor Archaeological Park; a UNESCO World Heritage Site which, thanks to Angelina Jolie's role in the Hollywood blockbuster, Tomb Raider, may also be one of the most famous – at least among adolescent males anyway. Regardless, you certainly did not expect the opportunity to indulge your passion for vintage automobiles, let alone a pair of absolutely mint Citroëns. Surely you'll be able to arrange a countryside tour in the 1931 C6 Limousine, but what would it take to get behind the wheel of that 1927 B14 Torpedo?

Kirimaya Golf Spa Resort | KHAO YAI | THAILAND

You simply cannot believe your luck. The course is immaculate and nearly deserted. The sun is shining brightly but without the intensity of midday heat and there is a light breeze blowing favourably over your shoulder and down the fairway. You're feeling confident this morning and you are ready to play straight and long. You decide to start your round on a high note as you press your tee into the turf between the markers usually reserved for professionals. On this 18-hole championship golf course, designed by Jack Nicklaus, that means you have just committed yourself to an incredible 7115 yards of technically demanding golf within the natural surroundings of Khao Yai's lush mountains. No problem, you think to yourself as you adjust your stance, pick your spot in the fairway, and start your backswing. Half a second later, the satisfying smack of titanium on plastic snaps through the valley as your first drive is launched down the middle of the fairway.

KIWICOLLECTION.COM

Amandari | UBUD, BALI | INDONESIA

"Agreed," you say after artfully negotiating an afternoon of perusing art galleries in exchange for… well… let's just say you'll both be very happy. It seems unbelievable that your villa, tucked away in the tiered rice patties overlooking the sacred Ayung River, is just minutes away from Ubud - the cultural capital of Bali. But it's true. And moments later you are greeted by the friendly smile of a gallery owner, without the slightest hint of pressure or pretense, inviting you into his studio. But you did not stumble upon this gallery by chance; no, you were begrudgingly given directions by the owner of that shamelessly expensive boutique at home. And now, you can hardly wait to hear him gasp when he sees you in a necklace identical to that preposterously overpriced one he proudly was displaying last week. Of course, you won't tell him what you paid for yours… unless he asks.

Alila Ubud | UBUD, BALI | INDONESIA

As a photographer, you've traveled the world in search of that perfect shot. When you arrive for a one-month tour of Bali, you are so captivated by the rich green of the Ayung River Valley, the infinity pool at Alila Ubud, and the not too camera-shy troupe of monkeys making tracks on your patio that you almost forget you're on assignment. Yet the call of duty must be answered. The next day, you set off with a guide to take shots of the island's central volcanoes, the village of Kintamani, and the beautiful scenery of Lake Batur. On the third day, you venture out solo, borrowing a bicycle from the hotel and riding into nearby Begawan village. You stumble upon what looks to be a festival in the making - women dressed in festival finery, young girls with big toothy grins balancing baskets on their heads, elders returning home to get ready. You stop, point, and shoot. It's a National Geographic moment in the making.

The Oberoi Vanyavilas, Ranthambhore | SAWI MADHOPUR, RAJASTHAN | INDIA
Your ten-day stay at The Oberoi Vanyavilas, Rathambhore was truly a unique experience. This special resort offered superb accommodations and stellar service, as one would expect from an Oberoi property. In addition to the main attraction of the wildlife safaris, there were plenty of other activities to keep you busy for a relaxing break from the hectic pace of most India itineraries. The spa services are excellent, the yoga classes are great, and you had a wonderful time learning to cook Indian food with the chef. The elephants on property, which were often sighted early in the morning, were the most magnificent elephants you had ever seen; clean, happy, gentle and very friendly. The service was on all accounts personally tailored to your own individual needs with a very hands-on management style that resulted in a thoroughly enjoyable experience.

COMO Shambhala Estate at Begawan Giri | UBUD, BALI | INDONESIA

You have returned home, from the three-day Anti-Aging Program at COMO Shambhala Estate at Begawan Giri, a new woman! The transformation began the moment you arrived at the airport in Bali, where you were greeted by COMO staff and escorted through customs to an awaiting car. From that point on, your treatment was first class all the way – so much so that you felt a bit like a celebrity (but without the paparazzi). Upon arrival at the hotel, you were assigned a wonderful "Personal Assistant" who anticipated your every need and gently ushered you to all your program's daily activities, including helping you navigate the rather impressive and overwhelming grounds. You have returned home relaxed and rejuvenated, and maybe just a little spoiled, appreciating the finer things in life.

Amansara | SIEM REAP | CAMBODIA

The hotel's ancient but stately Mercedes is reputed to have carried Jackie Kennedy. Perhaps. As it slips discreetly inside the compound, the metal gates automatically opening and closing, you feel as if you've entered a forbidden city, a secret kingdom for pleasure seekers and explorers. And indeed you have. For this is Amansara, a jasmine-scented world hidden behind lofty walls, yet close to the temples of Ankgor and the colourful attractions of Siem Reap. The chauffeur opens the door while a smartly-dressed man removes your cases and takes them to your room. So this is how it begins – the total service, the privileged attention, the exceptional hospitality. The brochure did say to expect five staff to every guest; what a tantalising prospect, what a perfect ratio for self-indulgence and cloistered contentment. Although history is beckoning beyond the walls, you're discovering the wonders of your own private temple. Angkor Wat can wait until tomorrow.

Four Seasons Resort Chiang Mai | CHIANG MAI | THAILAND

Overlooking the rice fields and the mountains of the Mae Rim Valley, the Four Seasons Resort Chiang Mai looms majestically above the mist and tropical jungle: perched on stilts, a graceful sentinel amongst the trees. The surrounding jungle blooms with bougainvillea and brightly coloured birds of paradise. Styled on a traditional Thai temple, the resort shimmers in the afternoon sunshine, a mirage of comfort and luxury set in naturally serene surroundings. This is why you have journeyed here, to escape into the mirage and dwell high amongst the trees in your private villa. The excellent Thai foot massage you receive poolside is another reason why you've returned and, naturally, you are looking forward to discovering how to create the perfect kaow soi gai, curry noodle soup with chicken, in Thursday's cooking class. Also, if you can drag yourself away from the lazy comfort of the daybed in your sala, you might make it to the Spa one of these days.

JUNGLE 245

BEACH

Aleenta Resort & Spa, Phuket Phangnga | PHANG NGA | THAILAND
After experiencing the frantic pace of Phuket's nightlife, and dodging the bronzed bodies scattered across Patong beach, you were ready for the privacy and seclusion promised by this contemporary hideaway. And, the moment you stepped into your ocean view loft, you knew this place was unlike any other beachfront resort you had experienced. Strong, cubic rooms, squared off with floor to ceiling windows and polished concrete floors created a compelling contrast to the soft blue ocean and to the wispy white clouds sweeping across the horizon. Delighted to find a fully loaded iPod Nano in the Bose sound system, you hit that magic white button and the room filled with the hypnotic beat of Ibiza inspired house music. You could feel the tension of partying in Phuket melt away as you slipped into your private plunge pool beckoning from the edge of your living room. This, you think to yourself, is exactly what you had been hoping for.

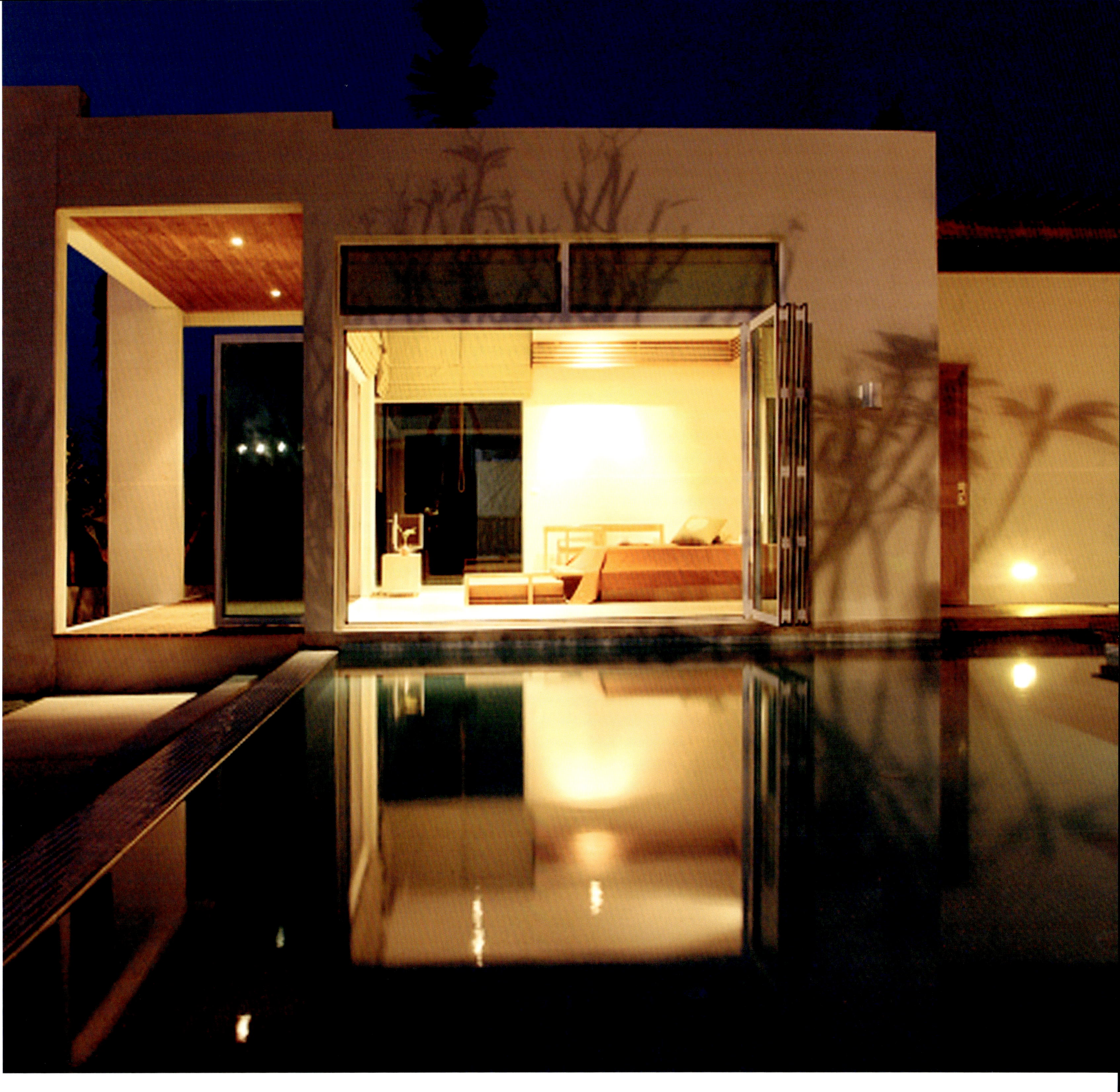

KIWICOLLECTION.COM

Evason Hideaway & Six Senses Spa at Ana Mandara | NINH HOA | VIETNAM

You are not looking to escape reality. Actually, you crave reality as long as it doesn't involve freeze-dried food or sleeping in a tent. The teak boat delivers you to your villa at the Evason Hideaway & Spa at Ana Mandara. You look out at the coral reefs, the rock formations, the miles of empty white sand beach to explore. The mountains of Nha Trang rise beyond your villa, and the South China Sea fills your vision. You don't say anything. There is nothing to say. You've found it. You explore the wooden walkways, meander through the gardens, admire the Vietnamese architecture. As you settle into your sunk-in pool, your butler serves you a glass of chilled blanc de blanc from your room's private wine cellar. That's fine. That is, after all, the reality you seek: the reality of pleasure.

Amanwella | GODELLAWELA | SRI LANKA

So far, the hardest decision you have had to make today was whether to have tea or coffee. But now, as you flirt with the bottom of your cup, you are faced with a real dilemma: do you wander back through the lush coconut grove and spend a lazy morning on the chaise lounger beside the private plunge pool flanking your contemporary suite? Or, do you finish breakfast with a few laps in the nearly olympic sized infinity pool that appears to blend seamlessly into the half-mile long crescent shape beach? Undecided, you opt for another cup of tea and commit to finishing this gorgeous plate of plump and juicy tropical fruit. You further resolve that no more questions are to be raised until you have read the sports section of the newspaper. After all, Champion's League is in full swing and you've yet to check the weekend's results.

The Andaman, Langkawi | LANGKAWI | MALAYSIA

You chose The Andaman, Langkawi for two very specific reasons, each equally important. First, the resort's location (situated between the majestic Mat Cincang Range and the deep blue Andaman Sea, and built in the middle of a virgin tropical rainforest) promises to be a spectacular diversion, and second, their offering of an activity filled "Kids Club". Because, let's face it if the kids aren't happy, nobody's happy, no matter how fantastic the scenery may be. Fortunately, the Kid's Club is proving to be everything you had hoped it would be. In other words, the kids are actually having fun without you, which means, each morning, you and your spouse can have hours of well-deserved, guilt-free peace and relaxation. And with the mini-cinema regularly showing children's movies in the afternoon, there just might be, on the horizon, a few more hours of peace for the two of you.

Chiva-Som International Health Resort | HUA HIN | THAILAND

It's just you and, well, you. There are no deadlines; no projects piling up on your desk; you are all alone. Upon arrival, you checked your phone at the front desk forcing yourself to let go and float, with the refreshing ocean breeze, through the health resort of Chiva-Som. Following the program individually designed by your personal Health and Wellness Advisor to suit your special requirements, you slip from the soothing interior of the water therapy suite and move to the treatment room. Lying back, you tingle as the lemongrass, citrus, and spice scrub invigorates your senses; drift off during the hot oil massage; and feel rejuvenated by the deep healing cocoon of the full body wrap. As the aromatic herbal extracts stimulate circulation and refresh your mind, you are left to ponder why you failed to schedule this getaway sooner.

Palazzo Versace | GOLD COAST, QUEENSLAND | AUSTRALIA

This would have to be one of the most superb places you have ever stayed. From the moment you arrived, until the time you sadly had to check out, everything was just so perfectly Versace! And like the brand, it was the subtle, but very noticeable nuances, that made all the difference. For instance, the entrance to the Palazzo Versace was filled with orchid stems during the day, but quietly changed to tea light candles at night. Stunning floral arrangements of proteas filled a lobby that had the understated elegance so typical of the Versace brand. In fact, everything, from the lobby through to the room, had the Versace stamp on it: the furniture, the linen, the cushions, the porcelain, and of course, the bathroom products. And from a European-style balcony, with an ornate rail, you overlooked the hotel pool and garden, as well as having a view of the fabulous Gold Coast.

The Legian | SEMINYAK BEACH, BALI | INDONESIA
Admit it. You were secretly envious when your friends, clad in their shiny black wetsuits, headed off to surf while you headed off toward university. Now, the master's degree long behind you, you're finally mastering the elusive sport of surfing, and are seeking out the best beach breaks in the world. Now it's Bali, where, right out front The Legian (of course, your hotel of choice), there are uncrowded perfect breaks, and a glorious swell rolling in from afar. Rising before dawn, you wax your board, and are out on the water before most of The Legian's other guests have even opened their eyes. Between sets, you glance over and swear you see one of your old college buddies, sitting on his longboard, grinning. A wave comes in. Grasping the board between your hands, you grin back and rise to take it.

KIWICOLLECTION.COM

Pimalai Resort & Spa | KOH LANTA | THAILAND

The hum of the waves rolling against the white sandy shore, the gentle sway of palm trees, and the blooming hibiscus flowers of Pimalai Resort were a mere dream yesterday. 24 hours ago, you were in the middle of a blizzard unsure if your scheduled flight would be cleared for take-off. Now, as you follow the chef's instructions at the Thai cooking class, you cheerfully toss sliced ginger, red chillies, and stalks of lemongrass into a sizzling wok. Add fresh prawns and a squeeze of lime juice. Another shimmer of the wok and your dish is ready to be craftily displayed on a bed of steamed Thai greens, garnished with a sprig of coriander. Taking a seat in the open-air pavilion, you savour your first bite; with a sip of crisp fruity white wine this culinary delight is complete. As the sun sets over the Andaman Sea you toast the perfect end to a dream day.

Namale - The Fiji Islands Resort & Spa | VANUA LEVU ISLAND | FIJI

Turning your face to the sun you close your eyes as the turquoise waters of the Koro Sea lap at your feet. You smile as you remember your reluctance to leave your watch, digital diary and laptop at home as your boss instructed you. Your anxiety around that decision is now simply laughable. It took only a matter of minutes before stepping onto Vanua Levu Island before you forgot about why you even needed them in the first place. The incredible natural beauty of the island and the warmth of the Fijian people were the first things that captivated you. Now it's Namale which you can truly credit with changing your life forever. Simply enjoying the truly breathtaking sunsets each day from the private deck of your Bures reminded you that there is so much more to life. Laptop? You can barely even remember how to spell it.

KIWICOLLECTION.COM

BEACH 259

The Nam Hai | HOI AN | VIETNAM

The rain falls, in steady silver sheets, from a sky that, only moments before was a blazing blue overhead. Bird songs fill the air from an array of species seemingly as multi-coloured as the bright unusual flowers: some orange, crimson, and blue; others a mixture of pinks and purples, glistening with each drop of rain that falls on their soft petals. While standing on the raised platform of your huge Nam Hai villa, you look across the three great pools to the white sands of China Beach. Through the quicksilver curtain you see the sun shining brightly over the Cham Islands and the South China Sea. Earlier, you immersed yourself in the unique culture of Indochina and experienced the humble lifestyle of the locals. Now, you wait in the shelter of your modern Vietnamese influenced style villa. The rain disappears as suddenly as it arrived. There, at the edge of the shore where the white sand meets the jade waters, a rainbow of tropical colours rises to the west. This is your favourite part of the day.

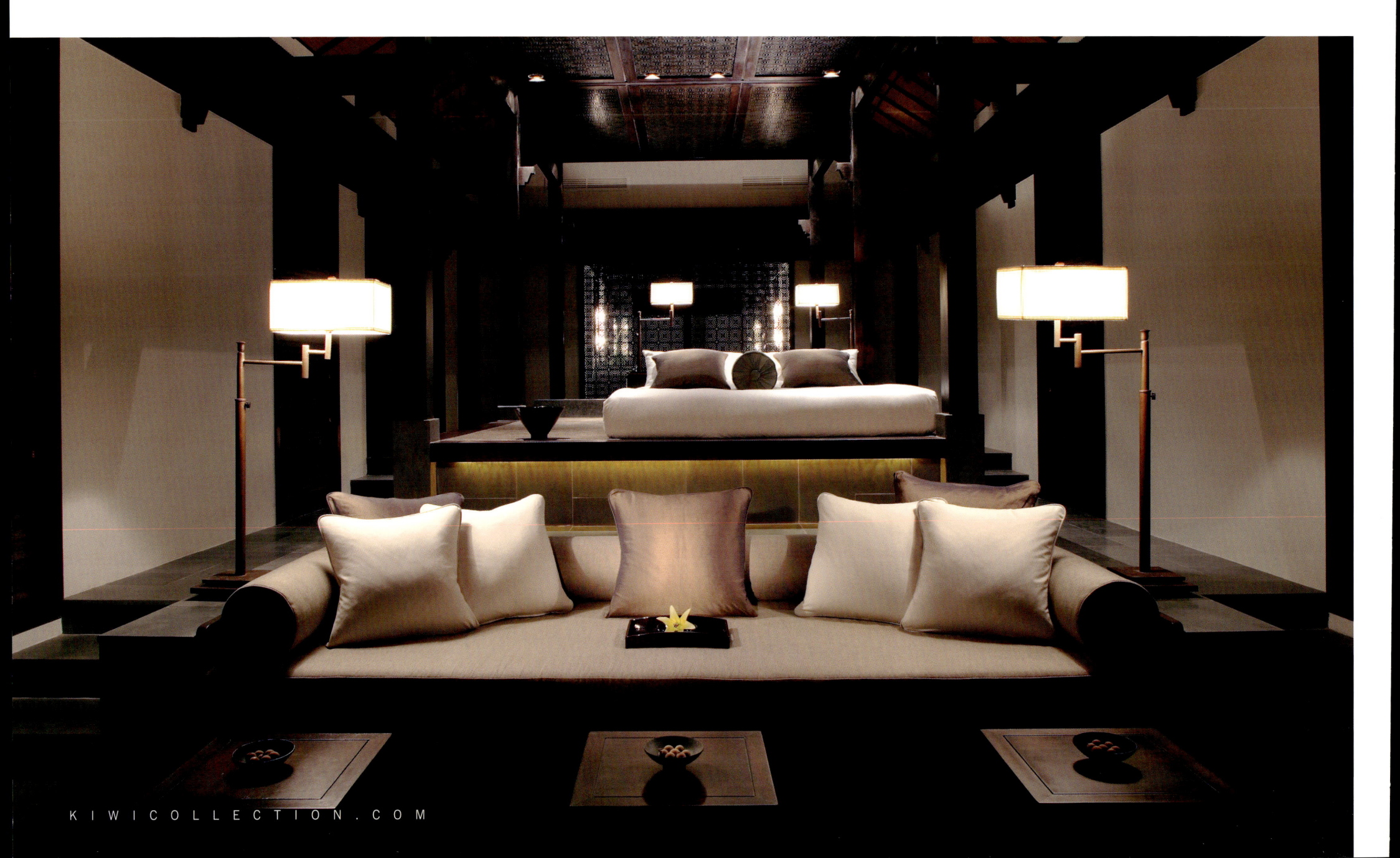

Vatulele Island Resort Fiji | VATULELE ISLAND | FIJI

After much research and plenty of discussion, you and your fiancé chose Vatulele Island Resort in Fiji for your long anticipated honeymoon. Once the decision was made it seemed an obvious choice, and four days into you ten-day holiday you couldn't be more pleased. Vatulele Island, with its famed eco-tourism and biodiversity, was certainly of appeal to the "outdoorsy" sides of both of you. And after yesterday's kayaking expedition from the resort beach to a local seabird colony (only twenty minutes away, yet as remote as the other side of the world), you feel more in tune with nature than you have in a long time. And, of course, being able to experience the great outdoors while being pampered at world-class luxury resort, is really what a honeymoon should be all about.

Karma Samui | KOH SAMUI | THAILAND

Betel leaves with grated coconut and pomegranates. Earlier today you splashed beneath a waterfall before trekking through the jungle back to Karma Samui. Tum yum steamboat of seafood with hot and sour dressing. Waves crash on the shore below, candles illuminate the night, and seashells decorate the wooden daybed. Green mango with crispy fish, lime, and lemongrass. Reclining beneath the stars, as you take a bite, your mouth explodes at the subtle blend of spices and fresh produce. Pheanang curry of beef cheek with chilli and Thai basil. From your villa's kitchen the chef approaches with another tray, the waiter steps in to discretely clear the previous course. A frozen concoction of mango sorbet, crystallised mint, and fresh guava is set before you, with two spoons. Ahh, dessert. Raising a spoonful to your partner's lips, you fail to notice the staff dissolve into the inky darkness of the night.

KIWICOLLECTION.COM

Karma Jimbaran | JIMBARAN, BALI | INDONESIA

"Amazing," you think to yourself as you lean back into the teak lounge chair and watch your grandchildren splash in the private pool of your four-bedroom villa. How did you manage to get your whole family here? And why did you wait so long to try? Your moment of quiet reflection is gently interrupted by a sharply dressed waiter who has come to double-check your dinner request for this evening. "Yes," you confirm, "no shell fish for the youngest." In an hour or two this private oasis will be transformed into a beautiful outdoor dining room. Music will fill the air. The sun loungers will be replaced with a table for all eight of your family. The children will be delighted by the flowers and by the candles set adrift in your pool, and your personal chef will create a sumptuous seafood feast on the barbeque. A masterful way to cap-off a perfect holiday – with the best part of your family tree.

BEACH 263

Sila Evason Hideaway & Spa at Samui | KOH SAMUI | THAILAND

Tonight the two of you are dining "on the rocks' at the Sila Evason Hideaway in truly one of the most romantic settings you have ever experienced. Dinner is, of course, traditional Thai fare, with the freshest of ingredients cooked to just the right spicy perfection, and presented in ornate serving dishes. Your own private dining table, adorned in immaculately white linens (how do they keep the whites so very white in Thailand?), has been set upon a platform seemingly floating above the tranquil blue ocean. The privacy of the moment is overwhelming. The only sounds are those of the waves crashing underneath and of a saxophonist playing in the distance. And the slow relaxed sigh of your partner. Or perhaps that was you?

BEACH 265

Anantara Resort Koh Samui | KOH SAMUI | THAILAND

What will you do today? That is your dilemma this morning. You raise your sleepy head from the magenta and gold Thai silk pillows, and blink in the honey light of the sun streaming through the open balcony doors. The sea breeze at Anantara is invigorating and fragrant, a seductive invitation to begin the day. To start, a breakfast of fresh tropical fruit that is bursting with juicy flavour, as you sit on your teak balcony overlooking the serene waters of Bo Phut beach. Next, a list of activities to fill your day: will you chose kayaking, deep sea fishing, golf, tennis, or perhaps a trip to the spa? You're right, too vigorous. Perhaps a lazy walk down to the beach, towel and lotion in hand. Alternatively, you could just relax and recline on the built-in sofa bed on your balcony, admiring the view as you contemplate life. Oh my, another day just like yesterday.

Tanjong Jara Resort | DUNGUN | MALAYSIA

The Gamelan music carried into your villa by the evening sea breeze gently wakes you. You've been enjoying your routine afternoon nap each day since you arrived at the Tanjong Jara Resort, and this day is no exception. In fact, the relaxation you've experienced at this resort is so paramount that you find it hard to recall one day from the other except for the vast array of distinctively different gastronomic experiences and spa treatments that have marked each day. After a day of swimming in the pristine waters of the South China Sea, you wake with quite an appetite. Tonight you've chosen to dine on your private terrace, with a butler bringing a magnificent Malaysian barbeque to you. You decide to take a bath before dinner and step out into your private tropical garden to fill the sunken bath with water. Your partner suggests you order some champagne. This is another routine you could get used to.

The Chedi, Phuket | PHUKET | THAILAND

If ever there were a country worth travelling to for the cuisine alone, it would be Thailand. Sure, on many occasions, you have dined in some of the better Thai restaurants back home, and thoroughly enjoyed your meal each and every time; however, your boyfriend always said afterwards that you really can have no idea how good Thai food is until you've eaten it in Thailand. You hate to admit it, but once again he was right. Starting with a mouthwatering meal of red curry chicken and spicy beef salad at Beaches restaurant in The Chedi Phuket (because on your first night you were just too tired to leave the hotel) and then working your way down the beach day after day for basil chicken, pad thai, and your new favourite dish, pomelo salad, this is certainly turning out to be one spicy vacation.

The Bale | NUSA DUA, BALI | INDONESIA

You both awake refreshed and smiling, your noses twitching as the aroma of baking pastries and freshly brewed coffee drifts on the ocean breeze into your pavilion. Holding hands, you follow the mouth-watering scents of breakfast through soothing white courtyards and past serene ponds to Faces Restaurant by the pool. Warm pastry in one hand, a steaming mug in the other, you listen as your fellow guests recommend the Beach Club just a short walk from the hotel to the secluded stretch of sun bleached sand on Geger Beach. There you can relax on sunloungers, overlooking the Indian Ocean and the beautiful Balinese Hindu Temple that looms above the treetops. A leisurely swim would be a great way to ease into your holiday. A tug of your hand and the flaky pastry you were holding disappears behind your partner's grinning lips. Luckily a fresh tray of baked delights has just arrived.

Angsana Resort & Spa, Great Barrier Reef | CAIRNS, QUEENSLAND | AUSTRALIA

What's that old adage? Opposites attract? Perhaps that's why the Angsana Resort & Spa proved to be such an appealing option for your honeymoon. When you consider it, the resort is a celebration of polarity. Angsana Resort is the meeting place between the longest coral reef in the world and the oldest rain forest in the world. The resort's award-winning restaurant, Far Horizon's, offers the best of indoor and al-fresco dining experiences. Activity time is spent either on top of the water: windsurfing, parasailing, and water skiing or under the water: scuba diving and snorkelling through the stunning Great Barrier Reef. Your idea of relaxation – a massage from the exclusive resort spa. Your partner's idea of relaxation – bungee jumping. Your experience at Angsana Resort & Spa confirms that there definitely may be some truth, and enjoyment, in that old adage.

Kempinski Hotel Sanya | SANYA, HAINAN | CHINA

Looking back on your decision to invite your Chinese counterparts to meet with you at your hotel, you marvel how such a simple invitation changed the course of the company's future. Things had been tense and, with no resolution in sight, you needed a break. You decided on the Kempinski Hotel, Sanya. Your only mandatory was relaxation. You left with a whole lot more. You received a message that your Chinese counterparts had demanded an urgent meeting. Only hours later, you found yourself meeting them in the Lobby Lounge at the hotel. Initially discussion was difficult; but then, it was as if the relaxing ambiance of the hotel's surrounds began to permeate the discussion. The spectacular views of the ocean, outside, were soon the focus and cocktails replaced the tea that had been ordered initially. Suddenly, they were willing to sign the contract that would save the company. They left that night, and you stayed another month.

KIWICOLLECTION.COM

Evason Hideaway & Six Senses Spa at Hua Hin | HUA HIN | THAILAND
You feel yourself floating on the warm tropical breeze, weightless, your heart beating in harmony with the day. Wooden bowls of fragrant frangipanis scent your peaceful hideaway just as did the peppermint scented mist blowing from large outdoor fans upon your arrival. The weight gently lifts from the pressure point in your shoulder and you feel the knot dissolve. Sighing, you continue to float on the massage table as the professional Evason Hideway Thai Masseuse kneads your back like delicate dough, the warmed coconut oil sinking deep into skin and tissue and aiding in the release of your muscles. Soon, you are a cloud drifting across timber bridges, your mind open to the beauty and balance of the natural environment all around you. Pausing in the doorway to the clay dome, you take a deep breath before entering the meditation cave at the Earth Spa, ready to continue your journey of rejuvenation.

BEACH

KIWICOLLECTION.COM

The Library | KOH SAMUI | THAILAND

Thailand's famous Chaweng Beach town is an electric and exciting place to be… for a few hours - the excitement was why you came several years ago. Here you are again, but with a totally different purpose in mind. You've done the obligatory visits to few old haunts, but of course they didn't live up to the memories. Now you've made good your escape to the pristine privacy of The Library. What a pleasure it was to find this stylish and upscale beach resort in this, perhaps unexpected, location. Small and intimate, the semi-minimalist concept of its architecture and interiors match perfectly with the taste and style you have grown to enjoy and appreciate so much. You grin to yourself as you think back on your earlier visits to this part of Thailand, and imagine how you would never have believed you could get so much pleasure from quiet sophisticated surroundings and a good book to wile away the day.

Alila Manggis | MANGGIS, BALI | INDONESIA

As the Balinese out-rigger cuts through the crystal clear waters, aiming for the Blue Lagoon and its magnificent coral reef, I look back towards the shore and Alila Manggis. The sun is warm on my face and a gentle sea breeze tickles my skin as I sip chilled coconut juice straight from the shell. In the distance, I watch as the trees of the coconut grove, that surround the thatched roof of my villa, dip and sway; the palm fronds dance in the sunlight; and the jewel-like, reds, pinks, and deep blues of the tropical flowers shine - bright blooms of colour in the lush greenery. Sitting up, I reach for the suntan lotion and take a deep revitalising breath of fresh salty sea air. Placing the bottle in my drawstring bag, I check my snorkel, mask, and fins; I can't wait to plunge beneath the cool water and discover the marine life living in the coral reef below.

Sea Temple Resort & Spa Palm Cove | CAIRNS, QUEENSLAND | AUSTRALIA

The sound of your children splashing, playing, and laughing in the safety and security of their very own knee-deep lagoon is an absolute delight. Their energy is a refreshing change from the emotionless drone of board meetings you had to endure last week. Shaking off thoughts of the office, you turn to watch the arms of your better half churn across the expansive pool in the middle of this impressive estate. In one fluid motion, you swing off your deck chair and dive head long into the crystal blue pool that is no more than five feet from your private veranda. Swimming with the grace and speed of the Great Barrier Reef's most powerful predator, you pop up from under the water in perfect position to intercept your partner in mid-stroke. Feeling confident, you suggest a race in the lap pool near the bar. Loser buys the first round and the winner picks the afternoon adventure. Either way, you win.

The Datai | LANGKAWI | MALAYSIA

You lead with a morning spent on The Datai's 18-hole championship golf course, where you can assist one another in improving your stroke play. Your partner counters with a session at one of the two tennis courts where you can both develop your backhand swing. You raise the ante with an exploring jaunt along the treks in the tropical rain forest, on a pair of mountain bikes. Your partner closes with an afternoon spent down at the private beach where you can lazily float in the tranquil waters of the Andaman Sea and watch the clouds drift across the azure sky. You play your trump: an intimate evening, just the two of you, on the balcony of your pavilion, candlelight and a bottle of wine, your closest neighbours are the monkeys, bedding down in the trees around you.

Amanpuri | PHUKET | THAILAND

After plunging into turquoise water, you leisurely stroke the short distance to the wooden pontoon offshore of Pansea Beach. Hauling yourself onto the deck, you take a moment to appreciate the pure beauty of your surroundings and to refresh yourself from the well stocked cooler box. 'Amanpuri' means peaceful place, exactly what you and your partner have discovered here at the edge of the Andaman Sea. Invigorated from your swim, you ignore the sprawl of sunloungers and creamy umbrellas set on golden sand and ascend the grand staircase that leads to the mysterious black granite pool and to the hotel. At your pavilion, your butler directs you to the spacious bathroom. Stepping out of the steaming shower, you are intrigued to see that the butler has laid out both your robe and a blindfold. Incense scents the evening as the soft sounds of a harp caresses your ears. Just what does your partner have planned for tonight?

Four Seasons Resort Koh Samui, Thailand | KOH SAMUI | THAILAND

You can't help but notice how much Koh Samui has changed since the last time you were here. Okay, that was several years ago but, still, the transformation is incredible. What you remembered as a rather quiet and undiscovered island now has become a major tourist destination. Which means: more people and crowds, certainly, but also a greater abundance of better quality shops, beachside restaurants, and high-end Thai spas. The main strip has become a busy and thriving street at all hours of the day and night, fantastic to visit, but just as nice to leave for the solitude and sanctity of the Four Seasons Resort Koh Samui. Discretely tucked away from it all on the hillside overlooking the Gulf of Siam, the hotel is but a short drive from the activities when the mood for adventure hits, although with paradise found, what possible reason would you ever find to leave this amazing resort.

KIWICOLLECTION.COM

BEACH 279

Amankila | MANGGIS, BALI | INDONESIA

You've worked more twelve-hour days in a row than you care to count. Now all you want is a nap in the shade. Your spouse, though, wants an adventure and you're too tired to resist. But when you arrive at Amankila, all is well. Maybe it's the three pools set into the cliff's edge, flowing one into another like terraced fields. Your partner heads off for the water palace of Tirtagangga, then takes the charge card to look for Balinese art in Klungkung. You stay in the library reading books. Your spouse rides a bike to the top of the volcano. You have ginger tea on the terrace. When a sailing trip is proposed, on a whim, you go along. Far out on the Lombok Strait, the wind at your back, you think, okay, more twelve-hour days like this wouldn't be so bad. Back at shore, you settle under a coconut tree. Eyelids closing, you finally get your nap in the shade.

Villa Beige | KOH SAMUI | THAILAND

Good morning, Angels. Given the exhausting nature and resounding success of your last mission, I'm sending you off for some well deserved rest. Your destination: Villa Beige, situated on Koh Samui, Thailand. This private cliff-top estate will provide the seclusion your desire. However, you will not be alone. I have arranged for staff and a private chef to cater to your every whim. Please also enjoy the villa's private spa facility. Their luxurious treatments will ensure that memories of your last mission dissolve. Of course, you will each have your own room with accompanying outdoor terrace. The travertine pool and Life Fitness gym are there should you wish to work at your fitness; though I suspect the magnificent ocean views from the pool and sun deck may provide a welcome distraction from your regular fitness regime. Angels, enjoy. I'll be in touch in the coming weeks with your next mission. Regards, Charlie.

Four Seasons Resort Langkawi, Malaysia | LANGKAWI | MALAYSIA

It all began with a conversation about Pulau Payar Marine Park's natural wonders. Or perhaps it was the tropical cocktails raised high to toast the victors of last evening's treasure hunt through the landscaped gardens of the hotel. The night simply slipped away at the Rhu Bar set on the edge of the beach, a skyscape of stars dancing above the gentle swell of the Andaman Sea. Lounging on the plump cushions of the sofa, you lost yourselves in a discussion with fellow guests concerning the rich flamboyant pirate history of Langkawi, a former tropical haven for marauding buccaneers. From cocktails to a nightcap neither of you notice the passing of the night, the lightening of the sky at the edge of the horizon, the gradual change of deep aqua waters to a bright jade. Comfortable on the Indian Mogul swing, your bare feet kick the sand, your pirate's bounty from last evening's treasure hunt asleep in your arms.

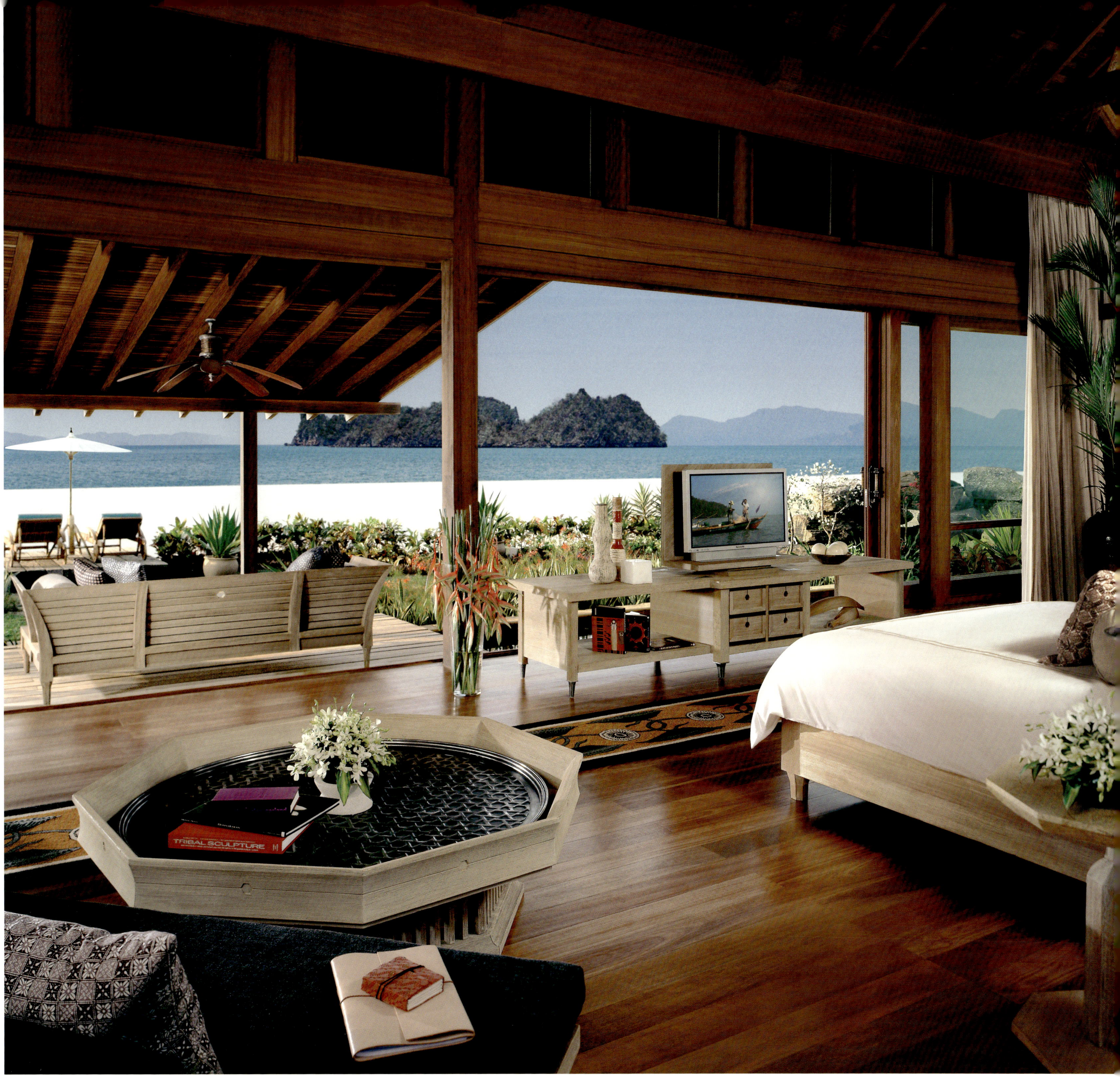
TRIBAL SCULPTURE

The Leela Kempinski Kovalam Beach | TRIVANDRUM, KERALA | INDIA

Lap – sigh, lap – sigh, lap – sigh. Ahh, there it is. Your breathing is perfectly synced with the lapping of waves on the beach. Now don't get too excited, it will only put you out of rhythm. It's taken a few days of 'decompression' to get your body relaxed and your mind calmed from its normal frenetic pace. You've been able to do this in no small measure due to the serene surroundings at The Leela Kovalam Beach. Sure, you've promised yourself to get some proper exercise later today; but later is, after all, a subjective term, and you're certainly not going to get yourself out of rhythm by stressing about it now. In fact, the only thing that might get your tempo off a bit is the dilemma you now face - deciding whether or not the tide will eventually get your legs wet to the ankles, or all the way up to your knees.

Aleenta Resort & Spa, Hua Hin Pranburi | HUA HIN | THAILAND

Once upon a time in a beautiful beachside retreat known as Aleenta Resort & Spa, tucked away from the other big hotel chains; where the staff always smiled and were friendly and attentive to every desire a guest might have; a man misplaced his cuff link, a sentimental gift from his wife. But before he had a chance to become upset, the smiling porter had organised a search of the grounds where it was thought to have been lost. Canapés and cocktails were served, keeping everyone's spirits high as they embarked on a starlit adventure through the lush gardens. When the gentleman reached into his jacket pocket for a handkerchief and pulled out the missing cuff link, with everyone laughing, the search was called off. The porter then led the man and his wife to a candlelit table and comfortable cushions on the beach. The waves crashed against the shore, the warm sea breeze caressed, as they enjoyed a delicious meal.

KIWICOLLECTION.COM

The Sarojin | KHAO LAK | THAILAND

As of this moment your goal is simple: settle in, settle down, and stretch out your seven day stay on this resort's ten lush and luxurious acres for as long as possible. And, lounging on one of those private pavilions situated in the centre of the pool seems to be the perfect place to see your plan play out. That is, until you meet Jowell – a man with the most unusual professional designation you have ever heard. It turns out that Jowell is an Imagineer. An architect of sorts. Someone who uses your imagination as a blueprint to build mind-blowing personal adventures. And, not surprisingly, Jowell is very good at his job. Because, in less than five minutes, he has convinced you that, as good as your plan to do nothing was, it could be greatly improved if you were open to the idea of doing anything you could imagine. And that is not an offer you get everyday.

The Ritz-Carlton, Bali Resort & Spa | JIMBARAN, BALI | INDONESIA

Breathe in. Breathe out. Your mind is focused on nothing more than the dramatic view of the Indian Ocean. A light breeze moves across your body as you complete your final yoga position. Stepping out from the pagoda, which is perched on the edge of a dramatic cliff face, you make your way to your private villa. Fortunately, this doesn't mean that you have to leave the ocean view that was just before you. You are intent on nourishing your mind, body, and soul. Each day, you've enjoyed therapeutic spa treatments, swam in the aquatonic seawater therapy pool, practiced your own yoga moves, and played golf at the hotel's exclusive championship 18-hole course. Whilst those activities are hardly a chore, with thirteen amazing restaurants to indulge in over the course of your stay, you're sure glad you've had the option of enjoying the more physical pursuits that make staying at The Ritz-Carlton Resort & Spa the complete package.

The Fortress | GALLE | SRI LANKA

My love. But I cannot call you that anymore. I cannot pull you to me, breathe in the scent of you, recite poetry from my heart. We are now separated and, I am, literally, in a fortress, though it is one to which even your cold heart would warm. The architecture is that of an ancient Dutch Fort, the interior a marriage of Dutch and Portuguese styles, with Sri Lanka touches that awaken the sensual. To cast you from my thoughts, I take swims in the turquoise pool, have high tea following a two-hour massage, am strengthened by the traditional Ayurvedic treatments. Thoughts of you grow weaker. In my suite's giant king-sized bed, I stretch out my legs for the first time in months. Awakening, I am calm, at ease. You no longer have hold over me. My heart has been captured by The Fortress.

Napasai | KOH SAMUI | THAILAND

Your personal assistant is notoriously good at finding hotels like this; knew you'd get weary of Bangkok and Chiang Mai, and want some quiet. Here at Napasai, there are no car horns, no beer bar discos, no guards blowing whistles; just the sound of the sea lapping the beach. It's a wonder - how did you possibly find an assistant who knows you so well? Smart, savvy, and truth be told, rather fetching as well. Restless, you take a midnight swim in Napasai's freshwater pool, so perfectly situated on the horizon it appears to flow into the turquoise sea. Perhaps it would be nice to invite your assistant next time. She deserves it. Your imagination wanders. But you pull yourself out of the pool and head back to the suite. Best to leave things the way they are. After all, good help is so hard to find.

The Leela, Goa | SALCETTE, GOA | INDIA

After a full morning in downtown Goa touring the many spectacular churches and Portuguese mansions that grace the city (including the famous Basilica of Bom Jesus, a World Heritage Monument that has housed the sacred mortal remains of St. Francis Xavier since 1695), you are happy to be in the air-conditioned car and headed back to The Leela, Goa for a little well-deserved "susegado" - the desire to unwind and live a little, starting with a 90 minute Ayurveda spa treatment to which you have been looking forward all week. The Health Spa at The Leela, Goa has the greatest philosophy: "Time stands still and a good time comes before all else". With mottos like that, one could certainly grow accustomed to the Indian lifestyle.

Banyan Tree Phuket | PHUKET | THAILAND

Beneath the shade of the banyan tree, two sun loungers stand side by side in peaceful seclusion. Golden sand gently slopes down to the water's edge, where ankle high frothy white waves give way to the shimmering swell of the saltwater lagoon. Exotic blooms of crimson, purple, and yellow border the path leading from your villa, at Banyan Tree, to the beach; their jewel bright colours reflected in the Thai silk sarong wrapped loosely around your hips. The sun is warm on your face as you step from the landscaped gardens onto the smooth sand. Your spouse is waiting, eyes shaded by dark sunglasses. "Promise me that your mobile will remain off." Sitting on the vacant lounger, you smile as an attentive waiter carrying a tray with two frosted glasses, a pitcher of mango daiquiris, and juicy papaya slices, sets everything on a small table beside you. "I promise, we are completely unreachable," you grin.

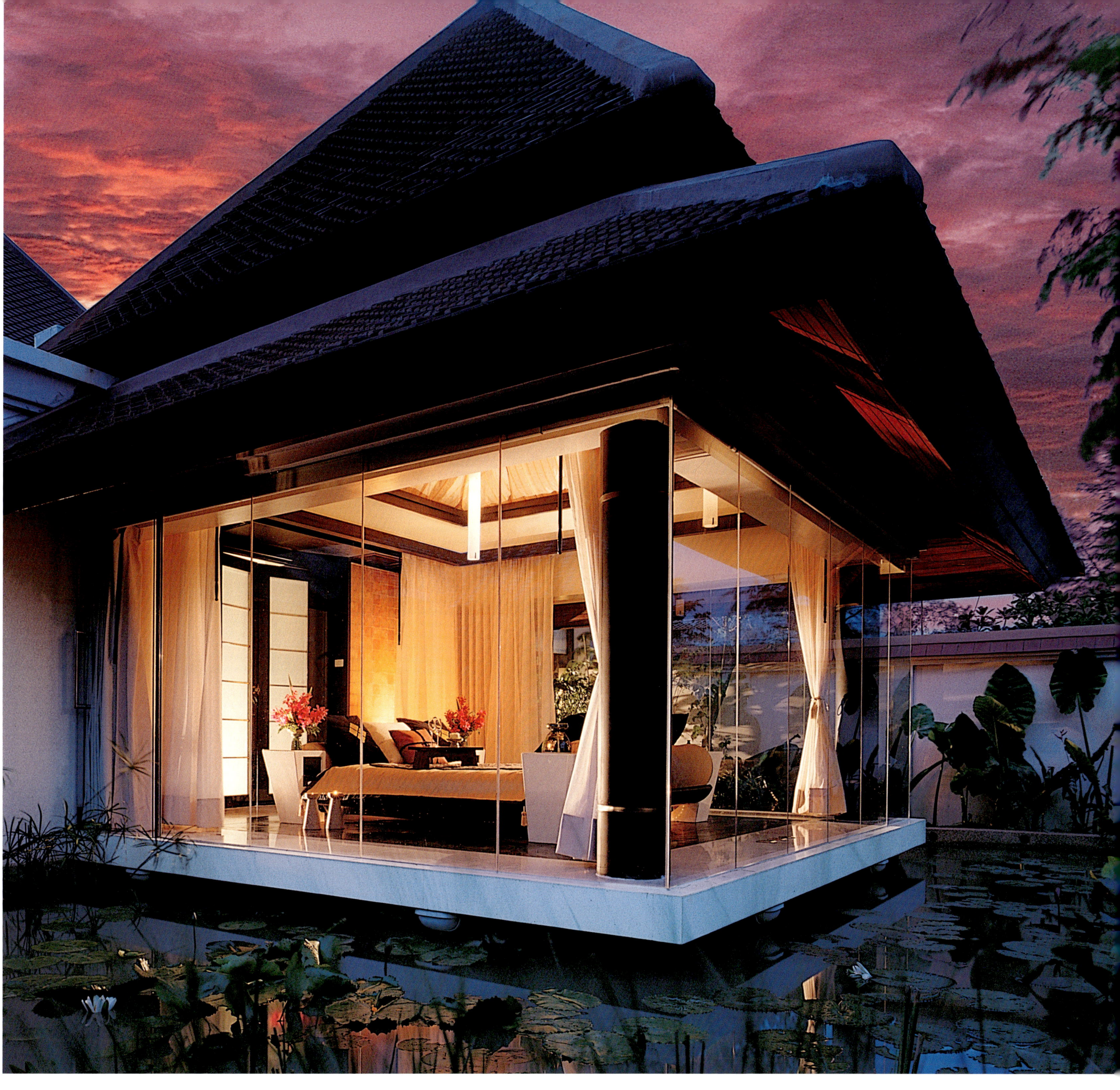

Banyan Tree Bintan | LAGOI, BINTAN | INDONESIA

Robinson Crusoe made his home in a banyan tree. As a child, it was fun to imagine sleeping between branches, the leaves sheltering you from the rain, frogs singing lullabies at night. Nowadays, unlike your favourite literary hero, you really don't want to spend 28 years on a remote island, encountering savages. Staying at the Banyan Tree Bintan, however, is just the ticket. It comes with the tropical forest and secluded golden beach. Your traditional Balinese villa is on stilts, complete with a resident monkey who visits every day around sunset. But just to make sure you don't turn too savage, there's the Greg Norman-designed golf course to keep things civilised. And a private chef to make Thai dinners each evening. That's the kind of literary fantasy that suits you just fine. And at the end of the day, this is one place from which you don't want to be

The Tongsai Bay | KOH SAMUI | THAILAND

Despite the attendant's reassuring nod and gestures of encouragement, you are not convinced. Sure the sparkling sea is calm and warm but that kayak is long, narrow, and tippy; and you've never been in a rowboat before, let alone a sea kayak. But now, standing up to your knees in the sea, with paddle in hand, you are ready to conquer your fears. Almost. Undeterred, the infinitely patient attendant demonstrates, once again, how easy it is to get on, and off, the kayak. Easy for him, anyway. Without hesitating, your vigilant assistant drags the unmanned boat a few feet away from the water. With a triumphant smile, he instructs you to sit on the beached boat. Laughing, you agree. No problem on dry land. As he skips to the stern, you feel a gentle push from behind and a tiny squeak escapes your lips, as you are set adrift on the sea.

Discovery Shores Boracay Island | BORACAY ISLAND | PHILIPPINES

Your brief – ultimate relaxation. Your challenge – a partner who works more than plays, who thinks sleep is a waste of time, and who tenses up at the thought of being in a relaxed state. The solution – azure waters and white beaches with sand so fine that it feels like treading on the softest silk. A dress code so relaxed that walking bare footed is the rule rather than the exception. A world-class spa which is sure to offer a treatment that will not only evoke relaxation and a feeling of well-being in anyone, but also have even the most ardent workaholic wanting more. A raft of aqua sports in which to participate; such as scuba diving, sailing, windsurfing, and kayaking. Stylish and contemporary accommodation with a private Jacuzzi and magnificent island views. The place – Discovery Shores, Boracay Island. The disclaimer – Discover Shores accepts full responsibility should your experience at the resort change your life and your partner forever.

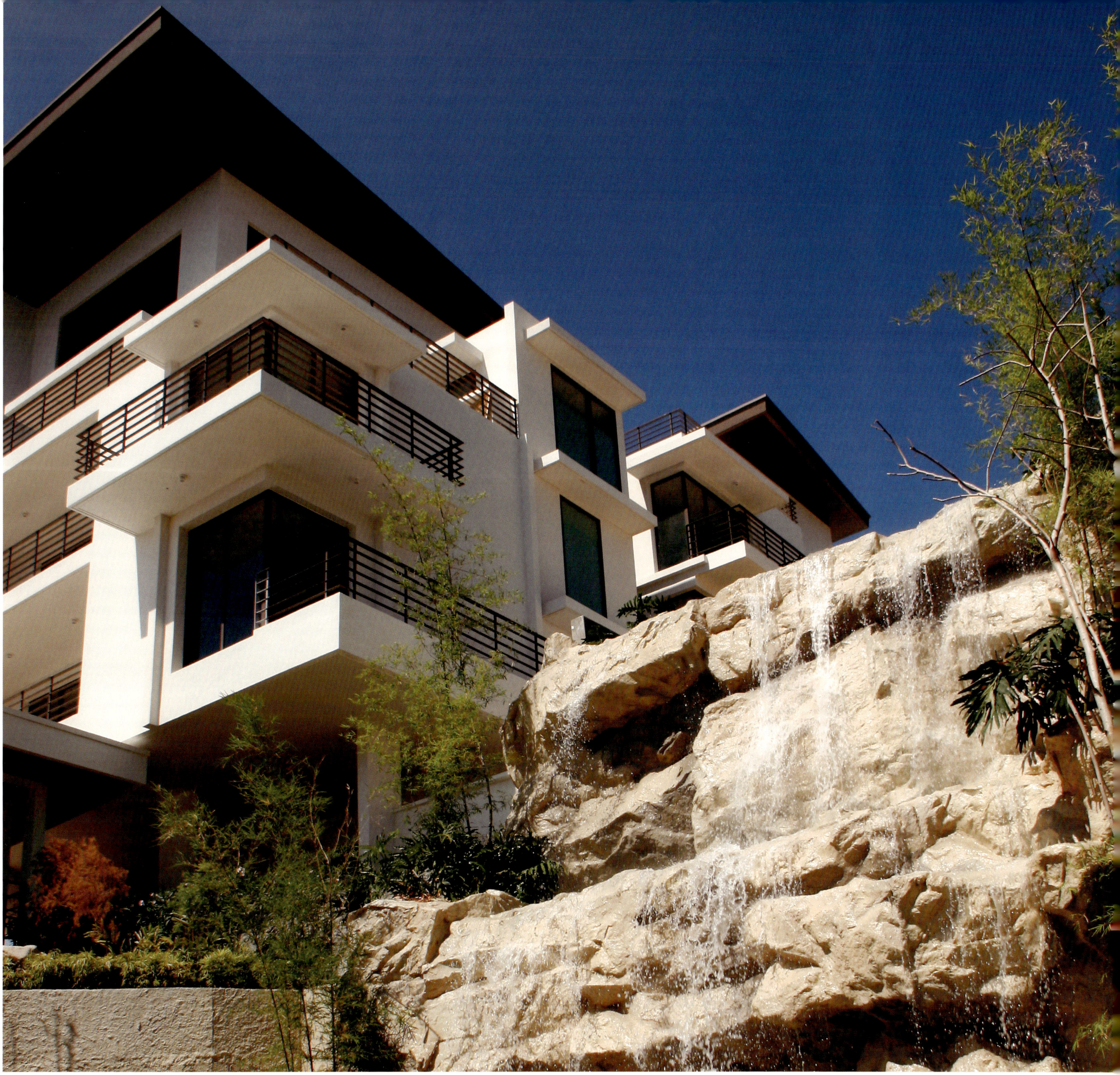

Trisara | PHUKET | THAILAND

They promised you a room with a privileged view. A room that looks out across the Andaman Sea. A room that catches the tropical breeze and where the soothing rhythm of the surf blends deliciously with the sounds of the forest. They told you to expect nature at your door, knocking gently and invitingly. They didn't lie. As you survey your private corner of Phuket, complete with your very own 10-metre infinity pool cresting the horizon, you know that the waiter was telling the truth when he translated the name of the resort from Sanskrit. 'Trisara,' he said with a broad smile, 'means the third garden in heaven. It's an island jewel, the garden of the gods, floating in a sea of beauty and tranquillity.' Everywhere you look, you see a picture of peace and paradise. Heaven indeed.

BEACH 299

index

AUSTRALIA

AUSTRALIAN CAPITAL TERRITORY

Hyatt Hotel Canberra - A Park Hyatt Hotel | CANBERRA 215
WWW.CANBERRA.PARK.HYATT.COM | +61.2.6270.1234

NEW SOUTH WALES

Burrawang West Station | BURRAWANG 73
WWW.BURRAWANGWEST.COM.AU | +61.2.6897.5277

Gaia Retreat & Spa | BYRON BAY 104
WWW.GAIARETREAT.COM.AU | +61.2.6687.1216

The Byron at Byron Resort & Spa | BYRON BAY 64
WWW.THEBYRONATBYRON.COM.AU | +61.2.6639.2000

Lilianfels Blue Mountains | KATOOMBA 89
WWW.LILIANFELS.COM.AU | +61.2.4780.1200

Capella Lodge | LORD HOWE ISLAND 41
WWW.LORDHOWE.COM | +61.2.9918.4355

Tower Lodge | POKOLBIN 90 + 91
WWW.TOWERLODGE.COM.AU | +61.2.4998.7022

BLUE Sydney | SYDNEY 130
WWW.TAJHOTELS.COM/BLUE | +61.2.9331.9000

Establishment Hotel | SYDNEY 146 + 147
WWW.ESTABLISHMENTHOTEL.COM | +61.2.9240.3100

Hilton Sydney | SYDNEY 184
WWW.HILTONSYDNEY.COM.AU | +61.2.9266.2000

Park Hyatt Sydney | SYDNEY 188
WWW.SYDNEY.PARK.HYATT.COM | +61.2.9241.1234

The Observatory Hotel | SYDNEY 204
WWW.OBSERVATORYHOTEL.COM.AU | +61.2.9256.2222

NORTHERN TERRITORY

Voyages Longitude 131° | AYERS ROCK 46
WWW.LONGITUDE131.COM.AU | +61.2.8296.8010

Bamurru Plains | KAKADU NATIONAL PARK 122 + 123
WWW.BAMURRUPLAINS.COM | +61.2.9231.2923

QUEENSLAND

Angsana Resort & Spa, Great Barrier Reef | CAIRNS 269
ANGSANA.COM/GBR | +61.7.4055.3000

Sea Temple Resort & Spa Palm Cove | CAIRNS 275
WWW.PALMCOVE.SEATEMPLE.COM.AU | +61.7.4059.9600

Shangri-La Hotel, The Marina, Cairns | CAIRNS 164
WWW.SHANGRI-LA.COM/CAIRNS | +61.7.4031.1411

Palazzo Versace | GOLD COAST 255
WWW.PALAZZOVERSACE.COM | +61.7.5509.8000

Ruffles Lodge | GOLD COAST 85
WWW.RUFFLESLODGE.COM.AU | +61.7.5546.7411

Hayman | GREAT BARRIER REEF 24
WWW.HAYMAN.COM.AU | +61.7.4940.1234

Voyages Bedarra Island Resort | GREAT BARRIER REEF 8 + 9
WWW.BEDARRAISLAND.COM | +61.2.8296.8010

Voyages Lizard Island | GREAT BARRIER REEF 29
WWW.LIZARDISLAND.COM.AU | +61.2.8296.8010

Peppers Spicers Peak Lodge | MARYVALE 74
WWW.PEPPERS.COM.AU/SPICERS | +61.7.4666.1083

Double Island | PALM COVE 19
WWW.DOUBLEISLAND.COM.AU | +61.2.9262.4838

Hyatt Coolum Ambassador Villas | SUNSHINE COAST 61
WWW.COOLUM.REGENCY.HYATT.COM | +61.7.5446.1234

Voyages Wrotham Park | WROTHAM PARK 55
WWW.WROTHAMPARK.COM.AU | +61.2.8296.8010

SOUTH AUSTRALIA

Thorngrove Manor Hotel | ADELAIDE 87
WWW.SLH.COM/THORNGROVE | +61.8.8339.6748

Punters Corner - The Retreat | COONAWARRA 117
WWW.PUNTERSCORNER.COM.AU | +61.8.8737.2007

TASMANIA

The Henry Jones Art Hotel | HOBART 213
WWW.THEHENRYJONES.COM | +61.3.6210.7700

The Lodge at Tarraleah | TARRALEAH 94
WWW.TARRALEAHLODGE.COM | +61.3.6289.1199

VICTORIA

Lake House | DAYLESFORD 108
WWW.LAKEHOUSE.COM.AU | +61.3.5348.3329

Adelphi Hotel | MELBOURNE 158
WWW.ADELPHI.COM.AU | +61.3.9650.7555

Crown Towers | MELBOURNE 168 + 169
WWW.CROWNTOWERS.COM.AU | +61.3.9292.6868

Hotel Lindrum | MELBOURNE 135
WWW.HOTELLINDRUM.COM.AU | +61.3.9668.1111

Langham Hotel | MELBOURNE 137
MELBOURNE.LANGHAMHOTELS.COM | +61.3.8696.8888

index

Park Hyatt Melbourne | MELBOURNE 152
WWW.MELBOURNE.PARK.HYATT.COM | +61.3.9224.1234

The Como Melbourne | MELBOURNE 164
WWW.MIRVACHOTELS.COM.AU | +61.3.9825.2222

The Prince | MELBOURNE 145
WWW.THEPRINCE.COM.AU | +61.3.9536.1111

The Westin Melbourne | MELBOURNE 157
WWW.WESTIN.COM.AU/M_INDEX.HTML | +61.3.9635.2222

Moonlight Head Private Lodge | YUULONG 83
WWW.MOONLIGHTHEAD.COM | +61.3.5237.5208

WESTERN AUSTRALIA

Quay West Resort, Bunker Bay | BUNKER BAY 81
WWW.MIRVACHOTELS.COM | +61.8.9756.9100

Chandeliers on Abbey | MARGARET RIVER 114
WWW.CHANDELIERSONABBEY.COM.AU | +61.8.9755.1100

Merribrook Retreat | MARGARET RIVER 110
WWW.MERRIBROOK.COM.AU | +61.8.9755.5599

Moondance Lodge | MARGARET RIVER 59
WWW.MOONDANCELODGE.COM | +61.8.9750.1777

Eight Nicholson Subiaco | PERTH-SUBIACO 128
WWW.8NICHOLSON.COM.AU | +61.8.9382.1881

BHUTAN

Amankora | PARO 68 + 69
WWW.AMANRESORTS.COM | +975.8.272.333

Uma Paro | PARO 75
WWW.UMA.COMO.BZ/PARO | +975.8.271.597

BRUNEI DARRUSSALAM

The Empire Hotel & Country Club | BANDAR SERI BEGAWAN, BORNEO 76 + 77
WWW.EMPIRE.COM.BN | +673.241.8888

CAMBODIA

Raffles Hotel Le Royal | PHNOM PENH 178
WWW.PHNOMPENH.RAFFLES.COM | +855.23.981.888

Amansara | SIEM REAP 243
WWW.AMANRESORTS.COM | +855.63.760.333

Hotel de la Paix | SIEM REAP 229
WWW.HOTELDELAPAIXANGKOR.COM | +855.63.966.000

La Résidence d'Angkor | SIEM REAP 235
WWW.RESIDENCEDANGKOR.COM | +855.63.963.390

Raffles Grand Hotel d'Angkor | SIEM REAP 224
SIEMREAP.RAFFLES.COM | +855.63.963.888

Victoria Angkor Resort & Spa | SIEM REAP 236
WWW.VICTORIAHOTELS-ASIA.COM | +855.63.760.428

CHINA

MUNICIPALITY OF BEIJING

Raffles Beijing Hotel | BEIJING 166
BEIJING.RAFFLES.COM | +86.10.6526.3388

St. Regis Hotel, Beijing | BEIJING 182
WWW.STREGIS.COM | +86.10.6460.6688

The Peninsula Palace Beijing | BEIJING 165
WWW.BEIJING.PENINSULA.COM | +86.10.8516.2888

The Ritz-Carlton Beijing, Financial Street | BEIJING 131
WWW.RITZCARLTON.COM/HOTELS/BEIJING_FINANCIAL | +86.10.6601.6666

Commune by the Great Wall Kempinski | THE GREAT WALL 50 + 51
WWW.COMMUNE.COM.CN | +86.10.8118.1888

Red Capital Ranch | THE GREAT WALL 72
WWW.REDCAPITALCLUB.COM.CN/RANCH.HTML | +86.10.8401.8886

HAINAN PROVINCE

Kempinski Hotel Sanya | SANYA 269
WWW.KEMPINSKI-SANYA.COM | +86.898.3889.8888

HONG KONG, S.A.R.

Four Seasons Hotel Hong Kong | HONG KONG 202 + 203
WWW.FOURSEASONS.COM/HONGKONG | +852.3196.8888

InterContinental Hong Kong | HONG KONG 126
WWW.HONGKONG-IC.INTERCONTINENTAL.COM | +852.2721.1211

Island Shangri-La, Hong Kong | HONG KONG 172
WWW.SHANGRI-LA.COM | +852.2877.3838

JIA Boutique Hotel | HONG KONG 149
WWW.JIAHONGKONG.COM | +852.3196.9000

Mandarin Oriental, Hong Kong | HONG KONG 186 + 187
WWW.MANDARINORIENTAL.COM/HONGKONG | +852.2522.0111

The Landmark Mandarin Oriental | HONG KONG 206
WWW.MANDARINORIENTAL.COM/LANDMARK | +852.2132.0188

index

The Peninsula Hong Kong | HONG KONG 153
WWW.HONGKONG.PENINSULA.COM | +852.2920.2888

MACAU, S.A.R.

Wynn Macau | MACAU 194 + 195
WWW.WYNNMACAU.COM | +853.2888.9966

MUNICIPALITY OF SHANGHAI

88 Xintiandi | SHANGHAI 197
WWW.88XINTIANDI.COM | +86.21.5383.8833

Four Seasons Hotel Shanghai | SHANGHAI 210
WWW.FOURSEASONS.COM/SHANGHAI | +86.21.6256.8888

The Portman Ritz-Carlton, Shanghai | SHANGHAI 212
WWW.RITZCARLTON.COM/HOTELS/SHANGHAI | +86.21.6279.8888

YUNNAN PROVINCE

Banyan Tree Ringha | TIBET 88
WWW.BANYANTREE.COM/RINGHA | +86.887.828.8822

Gyalthang Dzong Hotel | TIBET 101
WWW.COLOURSOFANGSANA.COM/GYALTHANG | +86.887.822.3646

Banyan Tree Lijiang | LIJIANG 54
WWW.BANYANTREE.COM/LIJIANG | +86.888.533.1111

ZHEJIANG PROVINCE

Fuchun Resort | HANGZHOU 78
WWW.FUCHUNRESORT.COM | +86.571.6346.1111

COOK ISLANDS

Pacific Resort Aitutaki | AITUTAKI 30
WWW.PACIFICRESORT.COM | +682.31.720

FIJI

Royal Davui Island Resort, Fiji | BEQA LAGOON 22
WWW.ROYALDAVUI.COM | +679.336.1624

Jean-Michel Cousteau Fiji Islands Resort | VANUA LEVU ISLAND 15
WWW.FIJIRESORT.COM | +61.3.9815.0379

Namale - The Fiji Islands Resort & Spa | VANUA LEVU ISLAND 258 + 259
WWW.NAMALERESORT.COM | +679.885.0435

Vatulele Island Resort Fiji | VATULELE ISLAND 261
WWW.VATULELE.COM | +679.655.0300

FRENCH POLYNESIA

Bora Bora Lagoon Resort & Spa | BORA BORA 11
WWW.ORIENT-EXPRESS.COM | +689.604.000

Hotel Bora Bora | BORA BORA 13
WWW.AMANRESORTS.COM | +689.604.460

Le Taha'a Private Island & Spa | TAHA'A 34
WWW.LETAHAA.COM | +689.608.400

INDIA

AJABGARH

Amanbagh | ALWAR 121
WWW.AMANRESORTS.COM | +91.1465.223.333

GOA

The Leela, Goa | SALCETTE 291
WWW.GHMHOTELS.COM | +91.832.287.1234

HIMACHAL PRADESH

Wildflower Hall | SHIMLA 94
WWW.OBEROIWILDFLOWERHALL.COM | +91.177.264.8585

KARNATAKA

The Leela Palace Kempinski Bangalore | BANGALORE 216 + 217
WWW.THELEELA.COM/HOTEL-BANGALORE.HTML | +91.802.521.1234

KERALA

The Leela Kovalam Beach | TRIVANDRUM 284
WWW.THELEELA.COM/HOTEL-KOVALAM.HTML | +91.471.248.0101

MADHYA PRADESH

Mahua Kothi | BANDHAVGARH NATIONAL PARK 222 + 223
WWW.TAJSAFARIS.COM | +91.762.726.5402

MAHARASHTRA

The Taj Mahal Palace & Tower | MUMBAI 141
WWW.TAJHOTELS.COM | +91.226.665.3366

NATIONAL CAPITAL TERRITORY OF DELHI

Trident Hilton, Gurgaon | GURGAON 174 + 175
WWW.HILTON.COM | +91.124.245.0505

The Imperial New Delhi | NEW DELHI 173
WWW.THEIMPERIALINDIA.COM | +91.112.334.1234

FOR DETAILED INFORMATION VISIT KIWICOLLECTION.COM

index

RAJASTHAN

Rambagh Palace | JAIPUR 162
WWW.TAJHOTELS.COM | +91.141.221.1919

The Oberoi Rajvilas, Jaipur | JAIPUR 109
WWW.OBEROIRAJVILAS.COM | +91.141.268.0101

Umaid Bhawan Palace | JODHPUR 62 + 63
WWW.TAJHOTELS.COM | +91.291.251.0101

Baghvan | PENCH NATIONAL PARK 113
WWW.TAJSAFARIS.COM | +91.769.523.2829

Aman-i-Khás | RANTHAMBHORE 111
WWW.AMANRESORTS.COM | +91.746.225.2052

The Oberoi Vanyavilas, Ranthambhore | SAWAI MADHOPUR 241
WWW.OBEROIVANYAVILAS.COM | +91.746.222.3999

Taj Lake Palace | UDAIPUR 97
WWW.TAJHOTELS.COM | +91.294.252.8800

The Oberoi Udaivilas, Udaipur | UDAIPUR 56
WWW.OBEROIUDAIVILAS.COM | +91.294.243.3300

UTTAR PRADESH

The Oberoi Amarvilâs, Agra | AGRA 193
WWW.OBEROIAMARVILAS.COM | +91.562.223.1515

WEST BENGAL

The Oberoi Grand, Kolkata | KOLKATA 127
WWW.OBEROIKOLKATA.COM | +91.332.249.2323

INDONESIA

BALI

Karma Jimbaran | JIMBARAN 263
WWW.KARMAJIMBARAN.COM | +62.361.708.800

The Ritz-Carlton, Bali Resort & Spa | JIMBARAN 288
WWW.RITZCARLTON.COM/RESORTS/BALI | +62.361.702.222

Alila Manggis | MANGGIS 274
WWW.ALILAHOTELS.COM/MANGGIS | +62.363.410.11

Amankila | MANGGIS 280
WWW.AMANRESORTS.COM | +62.363.413.33

Amanusa | NUSA DUA 107
WWW.AMANRESORTS.COM | +62.361.772.333

The Bale | NUSA DUA 268
WWW.THEBALE.COM | +62.361.775.111

The Legian | SEMINYAK BEACH 256
WWW.GHMHOTELS.COM | +62.361.730.622

Alila Ubud | UBUD 240
WWW.ALILAHOTELS.COM/UBUD | +62.361.975.963

Amandari | UBUD 238 + 239
WWW.AMANRESORTS.COM | +62.361.975.333

COMO Shambhala Estate at Begawan Giri | UBUD 242
WWW.CSE.COMO.BZ | +62.361.978.888

Four Seasons Resort Bali at Sayan | UBUD 233
WWW.FOURSEASONS.COM/SAYAN | +62.361.977.577

Maya Ubud Resort & Spa | UBUD 225
WWW.MAYAUBUD.COM | +62.361.977.888

Ubud Hanging Gardens | UBUD 226 + 227
WWW.UBUDHANGINGGARDENS.COM | +62.361.982.700

Uma Ubud | UBUD 234
WWW.UMA.COMO.BZ | +62.361.972.448

Bulgari Hotels & Resorts, Bali | ULUWATU 102 + 103
WWW.BULGARIHOTELS.COM | +62.361.847.1000

BINTAN

Banyan Tree Bintan | LAGOI 294
WWW.BANYANTREE.COM/BINTAN | +62.770.693.100

JAVA

Amanjiwo | BOROBUDUR 49
WWW.AMANRESORTS.COM | +62.29.378.8333

Alila Jakarta | JAKARTA 139
WWW.ALILAHOTELS.COM/JAKARTA | +62.21.231.6008

Hotel Mulia Senayan | JAKARTA 140
WWW.HOTELMULIA.COM | +62.21.574.7777

Kemang Icon | JAKARTA 189
WWW.ALILAHOTELS.COM/KEMANGICON | +62.21.719.7989

The Dharmawangsa | JAKARTA 144
WWW.THE-DHARMAWANGSA.COM | +62.21.725.8181

The Ritz-Carlton, Jakarta | JAKARTA 134
WWW.RITZCARLTON.COM/HOTELS/JAKARTA | +62.21.2551.8888

MOYO ISLAND

Amanwana | WEST SUMBAWA REGENCY 26
WWW.AMANRESORTS.COM | +62.3712.2233

index

JAPAN

Shiroganeya | KAGA 67
WWW.SHIROGANEYA.CO.JP | +81.76.177.0025

Gora Kadan | KANAGAWA 85
WWW.GORAKADAN.COM | + 81.46.082.3331

Tosen Goshobo | KOBE 52
WWW.GOSHOBO.CO.JP | +81.78.904.0551

Hinanoza | KUSHIRO 115
WWW.HINANOZA.COM | +81.15.467.3050

Hiiragiya | KYOTO 191
WWW.HIIRAGIYA.CO.JP | +81.75.221.1136

Hyatt Regency Kyoto | KYOTO 142
WWW.KYOTO.REGENCY.HYATT.COM | +81.75.541.1234

Iori | KYOTO 214
WWW.KYOTO-MACHIYA.COM | +81.75.352.0211

Kishoan | MATSUMOTO 48
WWW.KISHOAN.NET | +81.26.346.1150

The Ritz-Carlton, Osaka | OSAKA-SHI 196
WWW.RITZCARLTON.COM/HOTELS/OSAKA | +81.66.343.7000

Kuramure | OTARU 116
WWW.KURAMURE.COM | +81.13.451.5151

Seiryuso | SHIMODA 73
WWW.SEIRYUSO.CO.JP | +81.55.822.1361

Conrad Tokyo | TOKYO 199
WWW.CONRADTOKYO.CO.JP | +81.36.388.8000

Four Seasons Hotel Tokyo at Marunouchi | TOKYO 161
WWW.FOURSEASONS.COM/MARUNOUCHI | +81.35.222.7222

Grand Hyatt Tokyo | TOKYO 211
WWW.TOKYO.GRAND.HYATT.COM | +81.34.333.1234

Hotel Seiyo Ginza | TOKYO 137
WWW.SEIYO-GINZA.COM | +81.33.535.1111

Mandarin Oriental Tokyo | TOKYO 180 + 181
WWW.MANDARINORIENTAL.COM/TOKYO | +81.33.270.8800

Park Hyatt Tokyo | TOKYO 185
WWW.TOKYO.PARK.HYATT.COM | +81.35.322.1234

Seikoro Inn | TOKYO 156
WWW.SEIKORO.COM | +81.75.561.0771

The Ritz-Carlton, Tokyo | TOKYO 177
WWW.RITZCARLTON.COM/EN/PROPERTIES/TOKYO | +81.33.423.8000

LAO PDR

La Résidence Phou Vao | LUANG PRABANG 228
WWW.RESIDENCEPHOUVAO.COM | +856.71.212.194

Maison Souvannaphoum Hotel | LUANG PRABANG 182
WWW.COLOURSOFANGSANA.COM/SOUVANNAPHOUM | +856.71.254.609

MALAYSIA

Cameron Highlands Resort | CAMERON HIGHLANDS 58
WWW.CAMERONHIGHLANDSRESORT.COM | +60.3.2783.1000

Tanjong Jara Resort | DUNGUN 267
WWW.TANJONGJARARESORT.COM | +60.9.845.1100

Hotel Maya | KUALA LUMPUR 207
WWW.HOTELMAYA.COM.MY | +60.3.2711.8866

JW Marriott Kuala Lumpur | KUALA LUMPUR 136
WWW.YTLHOTELS.COM/PROPERTIES/JWMARRIOT | +60.3.2715.9000

The Ritz-Carlton, Kuala Lumpur | KUALA LUMPUR 151
WWW.RITZCARLTON.COM/HOTELS/KUALA_LUMPUR | +60.3.2142.8000

Four Seasons Resort Langkawi, Malaysia | LANGKAWI 282 + 283
WWW.FOURSEASONS.COM/LANGKAWI | +60.4.950.8888

The Andaman, Langkawi | LANGKAWI 253
WWW.GHMHOTELS.COM | +60.4.959.1088

The Datai | LANGKAWI 276
WWW.GHMHOTELS.COM | +60.4.959.2500

Pangkor Laut Resort | PANGKOR LAUT 36 + 37
WWW.PANGKORLAUTRESORT.COM | +60.5.699.1100

The Villas at Sunway Resort Hotel & Spa | PETALING JAYA 232
WWW.SUNWAYHOTELS.COM | +60.3.7492.8000

MALDIVES

The Rania Experience | FAAFU ATOLL 42 + 43
WWW.RANIAEXPERIENCE.COM | +960.674.0555

One&Only Kanuhura | LHAVIYANI ATOLL 10
WWW.ONEANDONLYRESORTS.COM | +960.662.0044

Cocoa Island | MAKUNUFUSHI 23
WWW.COCOAISLAND.COMO.BZ | +960.664.1818

Dhoni Mighili | NORTH ARI ATOLL 31
WWW.DHONIMIGHILI.COM | +960.666.0751

W Retreat & Spa Maldives | NORTH ARI ATOLL 14
WWW.STARWOODHOTELS.COM/WHOTELS | +960.666.2222

index

Soneva Fushi & Six Senses Spa | NORTH BAA ATOLL 35
WWW.SIXSENSES.COM | +960.660.0304

Banyan Tree Maldives Vabbinfaru | NORTH MALÉ ATOLL 27
WWW.BANYANTREE.COM/MALDIVES | +960.664.3147

Four Seasons Resort Maldives at Kuda Huraa | NORTH MALÉ ATOLL 38 + 39
WWW.FOURSEASONS.COM/MALDIVESKH | +960.664.4888

Huvafen Fushi | NORTH MALÉ ATOLL 28
WWW.HUVAFENFUSHI.COM | +960.6644.222

One&Only Maldives at Reethi Rah | NORTH MALÉ ATOLL 32 + 33
WWW.ONEANDONLYRESORTS.COM | +960.664.8800

Soneva Gili & Six Senses Spa | NORTH MALÉ ATOLL 18
WWW.SIXSENSES.COM | +960.664.0304

Anantara Resort Maldives | SOUTH MALÉ ATOLL 16
MALDIVES.ANANTARA.COM | +960.664.4100

Naladhu Maldives | SOUTH MALÉ ATOLL 20 + 21
WWW.NALADHU.COM | +960.664.1888

Taj Exotica Resort & Spa Maldives | SOUTH MALÉ ATOLL 24
WWW.TAJHOTELS.COM | +960.664.2200

MYANMAR

The Governor's Residence | YANGON 165
WWW.GOVERNORSRESIDENCE.COM | +95.1.229.860

The Strand | YANGON 138
WWW.GHMHOTELS.COM | +95.1.243.377

NEW ZEALAND

NORTH ISLAND

Lake Taupo Lodge | ACACIA BAY 70
WWW.LAKETAUPOLODGE.CO.NZ | +64.7.378.7386

Hilton Auckland | AUCKLAND 163
WWW.AUCKLAND.HILTON.COM | +64.9.978.2000

Mollies | AUCKLAND 145
WWW.MOLLIES.CO.NZ | +64.9.376.3489

Black Barn Vineyards | HAVELOCK NORTH 79
WWW.BLACKBARN.COM | +64.6.877.7985

The Lodge at Kauri Cliffs | KERIKERI 57
WWW.KAURICLIFFS.COM/LODGE.HTML | +64.9.407.0010

Lake Okareka Lodge | ROTORUA 86
WWW.OKAREKA.CO.NZ | +64.7.349.8123

Solitaire Lodge | ROTORUA 112
WWW.SOLITAIRELODGE.CO.NZ | +64.7.362.8208

Eagles Nest | RUSSELL 106
WWW.EAGLESNEST.CO.NZ | +64.9.403.8333

Huka Lodge | TAUPO 92 + 93
WWW.HUKALODGE.COM | +64.7.378.5791

Delamore Lodge | WAIHEKE ISLAND 82
WWW.DELAMORELODGE.COM | +64.9.372.7372

The Boatshed | WAIHEKE ISLAND 17
WWW.BOATSHED.CO.NZ | +64.9.372.3242

Wharekauhau | WAIRARAPA 84
WWW.WHAREKAUHAU.CO.NZ | +64.6.307.7581

SOUTH ISLAND

Grasmere Lodge High Country Retreat | CASS 95
WWW.GRASMERE.CO.NZ | +64.3.318.8407

Corstorphine House | DUNEDIN 65
WWW.CORSTORPHINE.CO.NZ | +64.3.487.1000

The Lodge at Paratiho Farms | NELSON 72
WWW.PARATIHO.CO.NZ | +64.3.528.2100

Azur | QUEENSTOWN 118 + 119
WWW.AZUR.CO.NZ | +64.3.409.0588

Eichardt's Private Hotel | QUEENSTOWN 96
WWW.EICHARDTSHOTEL.CO.NZ | +64.3.441.0450

Sofitel Queenstown | QUEENSTOWN 183
WWW.SOFITELQUEENSTOWN.COM | +64.3.450.0045

The Spire Queenstown | QUEENSTOWN 171
WWW.THESPIREHOTELS.COM | +64.3.441.0004

The Lodge at Tikana | SOUTHLAND 53
WWW.TIKANA.CO.NZ | +64.3.236.4117

Whare Kea Chalet | WANAKA 100
WWW.WHAREKEALODGE.COM/CHALET.HTM | +64.3.443.1400

Whare Kea Lodge | WANAKA 120
WWW.WHAREKEALODGE.COM/LODGE.HTM | +64.3.443.1400

PHILIPPINES

Discovery Shores Boracay Island | BORACAY ISLAND 296 + 297
WWW.DISCOVERYSHORESBORACAY.COM | +63.36.288.4500

Amanpulo | PAMALICAN ISLAND 25
WWW.AMANRESORTS.COM | +63.2.759.4040

index

SINGAPORE

Four Seasons Hotel Singapore | SINGAPORE 170
WWW.FOURSEASONS.COM/SINGAPORE | +65.6734.1110

New Majestic Hotel | SINGAPORE 213
WWW.NEWMAJESTICHOTEL.COM | +65.6511.4700

Raffles Hotel Singapore | SINGAPORE 144
WWW.RAFFLESHOTEL.COM | +65.6337.1886

Shangri-La Hotel, Singapore | SINGAPORE 154 + 155
WWW.SHANGRI-LA.COM/SINGAPORE | +65.6737.3644

The Fullerton Hotel Singapore | SINGAPORE 132 + 133
WWW.FULLERTONHOTEL.COM | +65.6533.8388

The Ritz-Carlton, Millenia Singapore | SINGAPORE 190
WWW.RITZCARLTON.COM/EN/PROPERTIES/SINGAPORE | +65.6337.8888

The Scarlet Hotel | SINGAPORE 157
WWW.THESCARLETHOTEL.COM | +65.6511.3333

The Sentosa Resort & Spa | SINGAPORE 47
WWW.THESENTOSA.COM | +65.6275.0331

SOUTH KOREA

Park Hyatt Seoul | SEOUL 198
WWW.SEOUL.PARK.HYATT.COM | +82.2.2016.1234

The Ritz-Carlton, Seoul | SEOUL 150
WWW.RITZCARLTON.COM/HOTELS/SEOUL | +82.2.3451.8000

W Seoul Walkerhill | SEOUL 148
WWW.WHOTELS.COM/SEOUL | +82.2.465.2222

SRI LANKA

The River House | BALAPITIYA 95
WWW.TARUVILLAS.COM | +94.91.438.2473

CASA Colombo | COLOMBO 200
WWW.CASACOLOMBO.COM | +94.11.452.0130

The Regency at Galle Face Hotel | COLOMBO 192
WWW.GALLEFACEHOTEL.COM | +94.11.254.1010

Amangalla | GALLE 143
WWW.AMANRESORTS.COM | +94.91.223.3388

The Fortress | GALLE 289
WWW.THEFORTRESS.LK | +94.91.438.0909

Amanwella | GODELLAWELA 252
WWW.AMANRESORTS.COM | +94.47.224.1333

Ceylon Tea Trails | HATTON 84
WWW.TEATRAILS.COM | +94.11.230.3888

Taprobane Island | TAPROBANE ISLAND 25
WWW.TAPROBANEISLAND.COM | +94.91.438.0275

TAIWAN

Les Suites Taipei Ching-Cheng | TAIPEI 205
WWW.SUITETPE.COM | +88.62.8712.7688

The Lalu, Sun Moon Lake | YUCHR SHIANG NANTOU 80
WWW.THELALU.COM.TW | +88.64.9285.6888

THAILAND

Rayavadee | AMPHUR MUANG 40
WWW.RAYAVADEE.COM | +66.75.620.740

Banyan Tree Bangkok | BANGKOK 212
WWW.BANYANTREE.COM/BANGKOK | +66.2.679.1200

Conrad Bangkok | BANGKOK 176
WWW.CONRADBANGKOK.COM | +66.2.690.9999

Four Seasons Hotel Bangkok | BANGKOK 129
WWW.FOURSEASONS.COM/BANGKOK | +66.2.250.1000

lebua at State Tower | BANGKOK 208 + 209
WWW.LEBUA.COM | +66.2.624.9999

Metropolitan Bangkok | BANGKOK 136
METROPOLITAN.COMO.BZ/BANGKOK | +66.2.625.3333

The Eugenia | BANGKOK 201
WWW.THEEUGENIA.COM | +66.2.259.9017.9

The Oriental, Bangkok | BANGKOK 167
WWW.MANDARINORIENTAL.COM/BANGKOK | +66.2.659.9000

The Peninsula Bangkok | BANGKOK 183
WWW.BANGKOK.PENINSULA.COM | +66.2.861.2888

The Sukhothai | BANGKOK 160
WWW.SUKHOTHAIHOTEL.COM | +66.2.344.8888

D2hotel chiang mai | CHIANG MAI 156
WWW.D2HOTELS.COM | +66.53.999.999

Four Seasons Resort Chiang Mai | CHIANG MAI 244 + 245
WWW.FOURSEASONS.COM/CHIANGMAI | +66.53.298.181

Mandarin Oriental Dhara Dhevi, Chiang Mai | CHIANG MAI 98 + 99
WWW.MANDARINORIENTAL.COM/CHIANGMAI | +66.53.888.929

The Chedi, Chiang Mai | CHIANG MAI 159
WWW.GHMHOTELS.COM | +66.53.253.333

index

The Rachamankha | CHIANG MAI 105
WWW.RACHAMANKHA.COM | +66.53.904.111

Anantara Resort Golden Triangle | CHIANG RAI 230 + 231
GOLDENTRIANGLE.ANANTARA.COM | +66.53.784.084

Four Seasons Tented Camp | CHIANG RAI 220 + 221
WWW.FOURSEASONS.COM/GOLDENTRIANGLE | +66.53.910.200

AKA Resort Hua Hin | HUA HIN 66
WWW.AKARESORTS.COM/AKA-HUAHIN | +66.32.618.900

Aleenta Resort & Spa, Hua Hin Pranburi | HUA HIN 285
WWW.ALEENTA.COM/PRANBURI | +66.2.508.5333

Anantara Resort Hua Hin | HUA HIN 71
HUAHIN.ANANTARA.COM | +66.32.520.250

Chiva-Som International Health Resort | HUA HIN 254
WWW.CHIVASOM.COM | +66.32.536.536

Evason Hideaway & Six Senses Spa at Hua Hin | HUA HIN 270 + 271
WWW.SIXSENSES.COM/HIDEAWAY-HUAHIN | +66.32.618.200

The Sarojin | KHAO LAK 286 + 286
WWW.SAROJIN.COM | +66.76.427.900.4

Kirimaya Golf Spa Resort | KHAO YAI 237
WWW.KIRIMAYA.COM/RESORT | +66.44.426.099

Pimalai Resort & Spa | KOH LANTA 257
WWW.PIMALAI.COM | +66.75.607.999

The Racha | KOH RACHA YAI 12
WWW.THERACHA.COM | +66.76.355.455

Anantara Resort Koh Samui | KOH SAMUI 266
SAMUI.ANANTARA.COM | +66.77.428.300

Four Seasons Resort Koh Samui | KOH SAMUI 278 + 279
WWW.FOURSEASONS.COM/KOHSAMUI | +66.77.243.000

Karma Samui | KOH SAMUI 262
WWW.KARMASAMUI.COM | +66.77.234.500

Napasai | KOH SAMUI 290
WWW.NAPASAI.COM | +66.77.429.200

Sila Evason Hideaway & Spa at Samui | KOH SAMUI 264 + 265
WWW.SIXSENSES.COM/HIDEAWAY-SAMUI | +66.77.245.678

The Library | KOH SAMUI 272 + 273
WWW.THELIBRARY.NAME | +66.77.422.767.8

The Tongsai Bay | KOH SAMUI 295
WWW.TONGSAIBAY.CO.TH | +66.77.245.480

Villa Beige | KOH SAMUI 281
WWW.VILLABEIGE.COM | +66.77.234.419

Aleenta Resort & Spa, Phuket Phangnga | PHANG NGA 248
WWW.ALEENTA.COM/PHUKET | +66.2.508.5333

Amanpuri | PHUKET 277
WWW.AMANRESORTS.COM | +66.76.324.333

Banyan Tree Phuket | PHUKET 292 + 293
BANYANTREE.COM/PHUKET | +66.76.324.374

Phuket Pavilions | PHUKET 60
WWW.PAVILIONS-RESORTS.COM | +66.76.317.600

The Chedi Phuket | PHUKET 268
WWW.GHMHOTELS.COM | +66.76.324.017

Trisara | PHUKET 298 + 299
WWW.TRISARA.COM | +66.76.310.100

VIETNAM

Park Hyatt Saigon | HO CHI MINH CITY 179
WWW.SAIGON.PARK.HYATT.COM | +84.8.824.1234

The Nam Hai | HOI AN | VIETNAM 260
WWW.GHMHOTELS.COM | +84.510.940.000

Evason Hideaway & Six Senses Spa at Ana Mandara | NINH HOA 250 + 251
WWW.SIXSENSES.COM/HIDEAWAY-ANAMANDARA | +84.58.728.222

roll

88 XINTIANDI 197	CAPELLA LODGE 41	GORA KADAN 85
ADELPHI HOTEL 158	CASA COLOMBO 200	GOVERNOR'S RESIDENCE (THE) 165
AKA RESORT HUA HIN 66	CEYLON TEA TRAILS 84	GRAND HYATT TOKYO 211
ALEENTA RESORT & SPA, HUA HIN PRANBURI 285	CHANDELIERS ON ABBEY 114	GRASMERE LODGE HIGH COUNTRY RETREAT 95
ALEENTA RESORT & SPA, PHUKET PHANGNGA 248 + 249	CHEDI, CHIANG MAI (THE) 159	GYALTHANG DZONG HOTEL 101
ALILA JAKARTA 139	CHEDI, PHUKET (THE) 268	HAYMAN 24
ALILA MANGGIS 274	CHIVA-SOM INTERNATIONAL RESORT 254	HENRY JONES ART HOTEL (THE) 213
ALILA UBUD 240	COCOA ISLAND 23	HIIRAGIYA 191
AMAN-I-KHÁS 111	COMMUNE BY THE GREAT WALL KEMPINSKI 50 + 51	HILTON AUCKLAND 163
AMANBAGH 121	COMO MELBOURNE (THE) 164	HILTON SYDNEY 184
AMANDARI 238 + 239	COMO SHAMBHALA ESTATE AT BEGAWAN GIRI 242	HINANOZA 115
AMANGALLA 143	CONRAD BANGKOK 176	HOTEL BORA BORA 13
AMANJIWO 49	CONRAD TOKYO 199	HOTEL DE LA PAIX 229
AMANKILA 280	CORSTORPHINE HOUSE 65	HOTEL LINDRUM 135
AMANKORA 68-69	CROWN TOWERS 168 + 169	HOTEL MAYA 207
AMANPULO 25	DATAI (THE) 276	HOTEL MULIA SENAYAN 140
AMANPURI 277	DHARMAWANGSA (THE) 144	HOTEL SEIYO GINZA 137
AMANSARA 243	D2HOTEL CHIANG MAI 156	HUKA LODGE 92 + 93
AMANUSA 107	DELAMORE LODGE 82	HUVAFEN FUSHI 28
AMANWANA 26	DHONI MIGHILI 31	HYATT COOLUM AMBASSADOR VILLAS 61
AMANWELLA 252	DISCOVERY SHORES BORACAY ISLAND 296 + 297	HYATT HOTEL CANBERRA - A PARK HYATT HOTEL 215
ANANTARA RESORT GOLDEN TRIANGLE 230 + 231	DOUBLE ISLAND 19	HYATT REGENCY KYOTO 142
ANANTARA RESORT HUA HIN 71	EAGLES NEST 106	IMPERIAL NEW DELHI (THE) 173
ANANTARA RESORT KOH SAMUI 266	EICHARDT'S PRIVATE HOTEL 96	INTERCONTINENTAL HONG KONG 126
ANANTARA RESORT MALDIVES 16	EIGHT NICHOLSON SUBIACO 128	IORI 214
ANDAMAN, LANGKAWI (THE) 253	EMPIRE HOTEL & COUNTRY CLUB (THE) 76 + 77	ISLAND SHANGRI-LA, HONG KONG 172
ANGSANA RESORT & SPA, GREAT BARRIER REEF 269	ESTABLISHMENT HOTEL 146 + 147	JEAN-MICHEL COUSTEAU FIJI ISLANDS RESORT 15
AZUR 118 + 119	EVASON HIDEAWAY & SIX SENSES SPA AT ANA MANDARA 250 + 251	JIA BOUTIQUE HOTEL 149
BAGHVAN 113	EVASON HIDEAWAY & SIX SENSES SPA AT HUA HIN 270 + 271	JW MARRIOTT KUALA LUMPUR 136
BALE (THE) 268	EUGENIA (THE) 201	KARMA JIMBARAN 263
BAMURRU PLAINS 122 + 123	FORTRESS (THE) 289	KARMA SAMUI 262
BANYAN TREE BANGKOK 212	FOUR SEASONS HOTEL BANGKOK 129	KEMANG ICON 189
BANYAN TREE BINTAN 294	FOUR SEASONS HOTEL HONG KONG 202 + 203	KEMPINSKI HOTEL SANYA 269
BANYAN TREE LIJIANG 54	FOUR SEASONS HOTEL SHANGHAI 210	KIRIMAYA GOLF SPA RESORT 237
BANYAN TREE MALDIVES VABBINFARU 27	FOUR SEASONS HOTEL SINGAPORE 170	KISHOAN 48
BANYAN TREE PHUKET 292 + 293	FOUR SEASONS HOTEL TOKYO AT MARUNOUCHI 161	KURAMURE 116
BANYAN TREE RINGHA 88	FOUR SEASONS RESORT BALI AT SAYAN 233	LA RÉSIDENCE D'ANGKOR 235
BLACK BARN VINEYARDS 79	FOUR SEASONS RESORT CHIANG MAI 244 + 245	LA RÉSIDENCE PHOU VAO 228
BLUE SYDNEY 130	FOUR SEASONS RESORT KOH SAMUI, THAILAND 278 + 279	LAKE HOUSE 108
BOATSHED (THE) 17	FOUR SEASONS RESORT LANGKAWI, MALAYSIA 282 + 283	LAKE OKAREKA LODGE 86
BORA BORA LAGOON RESORT & SPA 11	FOUR SEASONS RESORT MALDIVES AT KUDA HURAA 38 + 39	LAKE TAUPO LODGE 70
BULGARI HOTELS & RESORTS, BALI 102 + 103	FOUR SEASONS TENTED CAMP GOLDEN TRIANGLE, THAILAND 220 + 221	LALU, SUN MOON LAKE (THE) 80
BURRAWANG WEST STATION 73	FUCHUN RESORT 78	LANDMARK MANDARIN ORIENTAL (THE) 206
BYRON AT BYRON RESORT & SPA (THE) 64	FULLERTON HOTEL SINGAPORE (THE) 132 + 133	LANGHAM HOTEL 137
CAMERON HIGHLANDS RESORT 58	GAIA RETREAT & SPA 104	LE TAHA'A PRIVATE ISLAND & SPA 34

FOR DETAILED INFORMATION VISIT KIWICOLLECTION.COM

roll

LEBUA AT STATE TOWER 208 + 209	PENINSULA BANGKOK (THE) 183	SONEVA GILI & SIX SENSES SPA 18
LEGIAN (THE) 256	PENINSULA HONG KONG (THE) 153	SPIRE QUEENSTOWN (THE) 171
LEELA, GOA (THE) 291	PENINSULA PALACE BEIJING (THE) 165	STRAND (THE) 138
LEELA KEMPINSKI KOVALAM BEACH (THE) 284	PEPPERS SPICERS PEAK LODGE 74	ST. REGIS HOTEL, BEIJING 182
LEELA PALACE KEMPINSKI BANGALORE (THE) 216 + 217	PHUKET PAVILIONS 60	SUKHOTHAI (THE) 160
LES SUITES TAIPEI CHING-CHENG 205	PIMALAI RESORT & SPA 257	TAJ EXOTICA RESORT & SPA MALDIVES 24
LIBRARY (THE) 272 + 273	PORTMAN RITZ-CARLTON, SHANGHAI (THE) 212	TAJ LAKE PALACE 97
LILIANFELS BLUE MOUNTAINS 89	PRINCE (THE) 145	TAJ MAHAL PALACE & TOWER (THE) 141
LODGE AT KAURI CLIFFS (THE) 57	PUNTERS CORNER - THE RETREAT 117	TANJONG JARA RESORT 267
LODGE AT PARATIHO FARMS (THE) 72	QUAY WEST RESORT, BUNKER BAY 81	TAPROBANE ISLAND 25
LODGE AT TARRALEAH (THE) 94	RACHA (THE) 12	THORNGROVE MANOR HOTEL 87
LODGE AT TIKANA (THE) 53	RACHAMANKHA (THE) 105	TONGSAI BAY (THE) 295
MAHUA KOTHI 222 + 223	RAFFLES BEIJING HOTEL 166	TOSEN GOSHOBO 52
MAISON SOUVANNAPHOUM HOTEL 182	RAFFLES GRAND HOTEL D'ANGKOR 224	TOWER LODGE 90 + 91
MANDARIN ORIENTAL DHARA DHEVI, CHIANG MAI 98 + 99	RAFFLES HOTEL LE ROYAL 178	TRIDENT HILTON, GURGAON 174 + 175
MANDARIN ORIENTAL, HONG KONG 186 + 187	RAFFLES HOTEL SINGAPORE 144	TRISARA 298 + 299
MANDARIN ORIENTAL, TOKYO 180 + 181	RAMBAGH PALACE 162	UBUD HANGING GARDENS 226 + 227
MAYA UBUD RESORT & SPA 225	RANIA EXPERIENCE (THE) 42 + 43	UMA PARO 75
MERRIBROOK RETREAT 110	RAYAVADEE 40	UMA UBUD 234
METROPOLITAN BANGKOK 136	RED CAPITAL RANCH 72	UMAID BHAWAN PALACE 60-62
MOLLIES 145	REGENCY AT THE GALLE FACE HOTEL (THE) 192	VATULELE ISLAND RESORT FIJI 261
MOONDANCE LODGE 59	RITZ-CARLTON, BALI RESORT & SPA (THE) 288	VICTORIA ANGKOR RESORT & SPA 236
MOONLIGHT HEAD PRIVATE LODGE 83	RITZ-CARLTON, JAKARTA (THE) 134	VILLA BEIGE 281
NALADHU MALDIVES 20 + 21	RITZ-CARLTON, KUALA LUMPUR (THE) 151	VILLAS AT SUNWAY RESORT HOTEL & SPA (THE) 232
NAMALE - THE FIJI ISLANDS RESORT & SPA 258 + 259	RITZ-CARLTON, MILLENIA SINGAPORE (THE) 190	VOYAGES BEDARRA ISLAND RESORT 8 + 9
NAM HAI (THE) 260	RITZ-CARLTON, SEOUL (THE) 150	VOYAGES LIZARD ISLAND 29
NAPASAI 290	RITZ-CARLTON BEIJING, FINANCIAL STREET (THE) 131	VOYAGES LONGITUDE 131° 46
NEW MAJESTIC HOTEL 213	RITZ-CARLTON, OSAKA (THE) 196	VOYAGES WROTHAM PARK 55
OBEROI AMARVILĀS, AGRA (THE) 193	RITZ-CARLTON, TOKYO (THE) 177	W RETREAT & SPA MALDIVES 14
OBEROI GRAND, KOLKATA (THE) 127	RIVER HOUSE (THE) 95	W SEOUL WALKERHILL 148
OBEROI RAJVILAS, JAIPUR (THE) 109	ROYAL DAVUI ISLAND RESORT, FIJI 22	WESTIN MELBOURNE (THE) 157
OBEROI UDAIVILAS, UDAIPUR (THE) 56	RUFFLES LODGE 85	WHARE KEA CHALET 100
OBEROI VANYAVILAS, RANTHAMBHORE (THE) 241	SAROJIN (THE) 286 + 287	WHARE KEA LODGE 120
OBSERVATORY HOTEL (THE) 204	SCARLET HOTEL (THE) 157	WHAREKAUHAU 84
ONE&ONLY KANUHURA 10	SEA TEMPLE RESORT & SPA PALM COVE 275	WILDFLOWER HALL 94
ONE&ONLY MALDIVES AT REETHI RAH 32 + 33	SEIKORO INN 156	WYNN MACAU 194 + 195
ORIENTAL, BANGKOK (THE) 167	SEIRYUSO 73	
PACIFIC RESORT AITUTAKI 30	SENTOSA RESORT & SPA (THE) 47	
PALAZZO VERSACE 255	SHANGRI-LA HOTEL, SINGAPORE 154 + 155	
PANGKOR LAUT RESORT 36 + 37	SHANGRI-LA HOTEL, THE MARINA, CAIRNS 164	
PARK HYATT MELBOURNE 152	SHIROGANEYA 67	
PARK HYATT SAIGON 179	SILA EVASON HIDEAWAY & SPA AT SAMUI 264 +265	
PARK HYATT SEOUL 198	SOFITEL QUEENSTOWN 183	
PARK HYATT SYDNEY 188	SOLITAIRE LODGE 112	
PARK HYATT TOKYO 185	SONEVA FUSHI & SIX SENSES SPA 35	

MARY GOSTELOW   EDITOR

Mary has encyclopaedic knowledge of the luxury hospitality industry and an unparalleled global network of contacts. She is absolutely passionate about hotels, luxury, quality, people – and giving the most to life.

An inveterate traveller, she is Owner and President of The Gostelow Report, essential monthly market intelligence briefing for the top levels of the hospitality industry. She is also Contributing Editor to *Elite Traveler*, The Private Jet Lifestyle Magazine, *EnRoute* and *HOTELS*, plus she has regular columns in such publications as *Agent@Home*, *CNBC Europe*, *IN-LAN*, *Lexpert*, and *Le Magazine*. She has an honorary degree from Johnson & Wales University.

As a partner in Kiwi Collection Inc. Mary Gostelow is the Editor in Chief of our online luxury travel magazine *WOW.travel* and Editor of our award-winning coffee table book series *Overnight Sensations*, published by Kiwi Collection.

VICTORIA BUSHNELL   CONTRIBUTING WRITER

One parent was a geologist. The other was in the music industry. Sufficed to say, Victoria grew up with a good understanding of the numerous professional opportunities awaiting a bright young woman growing up in Los Angeles. So naturally she chose to become a writer. Her career started as a reporter for a handful of entertainment trade magazine, before she took a gig working as a stringer for the *Hollywood Reporter*. Her passion for writing motivated her to try a variety of writing styles and she found that, along with sharp reporting skills, she also had a knack for writing short fiction.

Since then she has written a guidebook, published numerous short stories, and worked extensively as a film and travel writer.

A self-confessed grammar snob, she also works as an editor smoothing the edges off the hurried work of journeymen writers, reporters, publicists, and marketing professionals.

NATALIE EVANS   CONTRIBUTING WRITER

By day, Natalie Evans operates under the cover of an advertising executive; but by night, indulges in her true passion, travel writing. Her most notable missions have included trips to Europe – France, Spain, Portugal, Italy, Austria, and the United Kingdom; Asia – Vietnam, Thailand, Indonesia, and Lao PDR; and a lone state of America – Hawaii.

Natalie's love of food and wine is counterbalanced with her keen interest in physical pursuits. This includes anything from lifting content (nor sane) unless she has some travel plans on her horizon. Having just returned from a trip to Margaret River in Western Australia, and with a trip to Darwin in Australia's outback and to New York later this year, it seems Natalie might stay sane for a while.

ELINA FURMAN   CONTRIBUTING WRITER

Elina's passion for travel took seed while working as an editor, online, at *Travel Holiday*. Since then, her contribution to numerous travel and lifestyle publications like *The Knot*, *Tango*, *Nikki Style*, *Ocean Style*, and others has helped her career as a writer blossom. Most recently, her experience in the travel industry earned her a job helping a major hotel company brand two of their internationally recognised luxury holiday properties.

Based in Manhattan, Elina has enjoyed a prolific freelance career that has seen her through more than 20 books, including her latest *Boomerang Nation* and *Kiss and Run* (the first book about female commitment phobia).

Through her work as a media expert and author, she has appeared on over 100 national and local television and radio shows, such as *The Today Show*, *Good Morning America*, and *Geraldo at Large*.

SALLY HAXTHOW   CONTRIBUTING WRITER

One thing you should know about Sally is that there are two Sallys. One is creative, with a long list of awards in the world of literary fiction writing; the other is corporate, with a proven track record in the world of business.

In the past few years, Sally has earned, for her short stories, numerous top honours from North American and international zines and anthologies. This success has come as a sideline to a professional career where, in a senior executive role, she applies her communications and business development acumen to help emerging companies prosper.

Through both business and personal pursuits, her passport has earned its share of customs stamps over the years. Should you find yourself on a plane seated next to her, on the way to some exotic locale, be sure to ask her for both of her business cards.

BEN HUDSON   CONTRIBUTING WRITER

Unlike most writers Ben has no desire to write the next great novel. In fact, over the last ten years he hasn't written anything longer than a page and is loathed to try. Ironically this frank confession has helped him secure numerous freelance writing jobs with a variety of boutique advertising agencies. He's an award winning advertising copywriter who has helped countless marketing professionals communicate their (mostly) great ideas in short and simple language and had a fantastic time doing it.

Before unearthing his knack with the alphabet Ben was dangerously close to enrolling in a large Law School in eastern Canada. But unable to bare the thought of missing a ski season he declined—possibly one of the best decisions of his life, because he quickly discovered that one could earn a decent living working as a writer with no desire to write a book.

SEAN MARTIN   CONTRIBUTING WRITER

Born in a mud hut in Kenya and raised on a sugar cane plantation in South Africa, Sean matured into a talented writer and photographer in Brussels, and now mellows in London, England. Sean's life has followed many paths and compass points. And, while he is still unsure what he wants to be when he grows up, writing and photography have been consistent waypoints that have kept him on track throughout the journey.

Over the last 20 years he has worked in copywriting, editing, and marketing roles for a wide range of publications and organisations. He likes nothing better than a blank screen, a creative challenge, and an accommodating deadline. Where would he like to be ten years from now? Living in the South of France, the sun over his shoulder and the Mediterranean ahead, writing his second bestseller.

LEISA A. SZCZEPANSKI   CONTRIBUTING WRITER

Live beneath a golden sun and dance, sing, and love your way through life: a beautiful philosophy Leisa learned growing up on the beaches beside the tropical waters of the Pacific Ocean.

Despite an undergraduate degree and the constant threat of a full time job, Leisa found the call of distant shores impossible to resist. Eventually, she succumbed to the pressure of her adventurous spirit and set off on a series of international adventures, with journal in hand and a plan to write a wonderful novel.

Leisa claims that her best research is done when she's the last person left dancing beneath the stars and the first person up to greet the sun. She likes to sing along to her favourite songs when nobody is around or when the music is really loud, so that no one is offended by her off pitch tone.

photo credits

Alila Jakarta
photos courtesy of
ALILA HOTELS & RESORTS

page 139

Alila Manggis
photos courtesy of
ALILA HOTELS & RESORTS

page 274

Alila Ubud
photos courtesy of
ALILA HOTELS & RESORTS

page 240

Four Seasons Hotel Bangkok
photos courtesy of
ROBERT MILLER
www.robertmillerpictures.com

page 129

Four Seasons Hotel Hong Kong
photos courtesy of
MARKUS GORTZ
www.markusgortz.com

page 202 + 203

Four Seasons Hotel Shanghai
photos courtesy of
ROBERT MILLER
www.robertmillerpictures.com

page 210

Four Seasons Hotel Singapore
photos courtesy of
ROBERT MILLER
www.robertmillerpictures.com

page 170

Four Seasons Hotel Tokyo at Marunouchi
photos courtesy of
ROBERT MILLER
www.robertmillerpictures.com

page 161

Four Seasons Resort Bali at Sayan
photos courtesy of
PETER MEALIN
PETER MEALIN PHOTOGRAPHY
petermealin@pacific.net.sg

photos courtesy of
CHRIS CYPERT

page 233

Four Seasons Resort Chiang Mai
photos courtesy of
ROBERT MILLER
www.robertmillerpictures.com

page 244 + 245

Four Seasons Resort Koh Samui, Thailand
photos courtesy of
MARKUS GORTZ
www.markusgortz.com

page 278 + 279

Four Seasons Resort Langkawi, Malaysia
photos courtesy of
MARKUS GORTZ
www.markusgortz.com

page 282 + 283

Four Seasons Resort Maldives at Kuda Huraa
photos courtesy of
MARKUS GORTZ
www.markusgortz.com

page 38 + 39

Four Seasons Tented Camp Golden Triangle, Thailand
photos courtesy of
MARKUS GORTZ
www.markusgortz.com

page 220 + 221

acknowledgements & copyright

PUBLISHERS
PHILIPPE KJELLGREN
BRIAN MUMBY

EDITOR
MARY GOSTELOW

CONCEPT & ART DIRECTION
PHILIPPE KJELLGREN

DESIGN
JULIA KAPLUN
KIM WOLF

PRODUCTION & LAYOUT
EUGENE CHEKANOV
ASHLEY DUFEK
JOAN HUNTER
JULIA KAPLUN

HEAD OF RESEARCH
BRADLEY COCKS

RESEARCH
BRADLEY COCKS
RACHEL DENNING
MARY GOSTELOW
ERIK HAUGEN
PHILIPPE KJELLGREN
DEBRA MCKENZIE
JOHN NIELSEN
SHOJI YAMAMOTO

EDITORIAL COORDINATION
BRIAN MUMBY

TEXT & COPYWRITING
GEOFFREY BIRD
BEN HUDSON

CONTRIBUTNG WRITERS
VICTORIA BUSHNELL
NATALIE EVANS
ELINA FURMAN
SALLY HAXTHOW
BEN HUDSON
SEAN MARTIN
LEISA A. SZCZEPANSKI

ENGLISH COPYEDITING
SYLVIA RAYER

IMAGE CONTROL
KAREN MUMBY

EDITING
ASHLEY DUFEK
KAREN MUMBY

QUALITY CONTROL
EUGENE CHEKANOV
ASHLEY DUFEK
JOAN HUNTER
JULIA KAPLUN
KAREN MUMBY
VER PESARILLO

COVER & END SHEET DESIGN
HANNES OTTAHAL
KIM WOLF

KIWI COVER & END SHEET PHOTOGRAPH BY
©2003 ROBERT KAUFMAN
WWW.SILVERVISIONS.COM

ONLINE DESIGN & DEVELOPMENT
RICHARD BILLIS
PETER JUBB
HANNES OTTAHAL
TYLER PAYNE

INVALUABLE SUPPORT
PER BRILLIOTH
MATS CARLSSON
ASHLEY HEPPENSTALL
LUKAS LUNDIN
ALEX SCHÜTZ
DATO' MARK YEOH SEOK KAH

In addition a special thank you to all the participating properties, their Owners, Staff, Public Relations Companies and of course, our mascot Ransom.

kiwi COLLECTION®

OVERNIGHT SENSATIONS ASIA PACIFIC

Copyright © 2007 Kiwi Collection Inc.

07 08 09 10 11   9 8 7 6 5 4 3 2 1

All right reserved. No part of this book may be reproduced, stored in a retrieval system or transmitted in any form or by any means without the prior written permission of the Publishers.

PUBLISHED BY
KIWI COLLECTION INC
KIWI COLLECTION INC
#301, 993 WEST 8TH AVENUE
VANCOUVER, BC V5Z 1E4
CANADA

ISBN 978-0-9735989-4-0

Printed & Bound in Singapore by
C S GRAPHICS PTE LTD

Colour Separation
IO COLOR, LLP

KIWICOLLECTION.COM

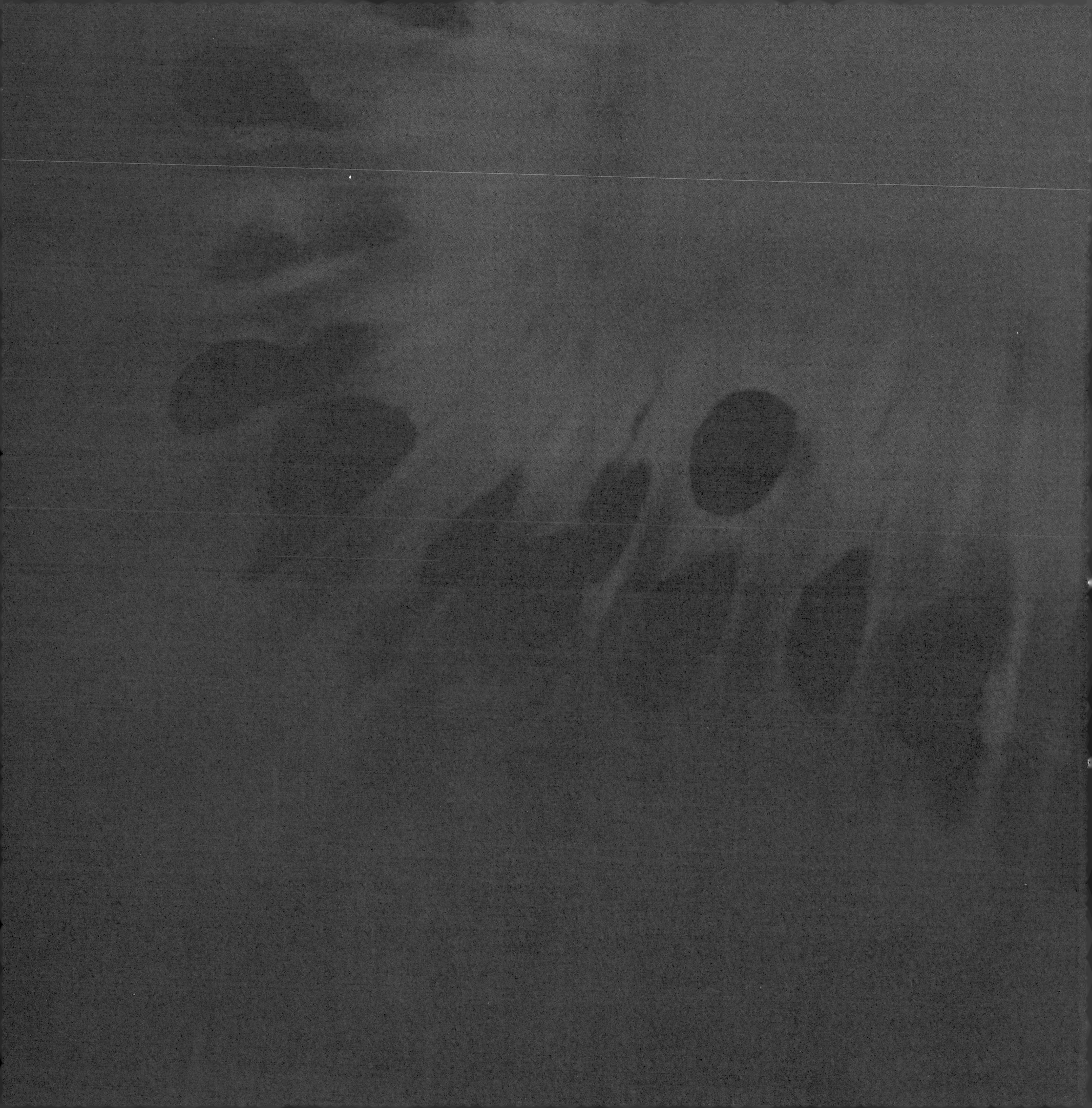